REAL WAGES IN MANUFACTURING

1890–1914

NATIONAL BUREAU OF ECONOMIC RESEARCH
NUMBER 70, GENERAL SERIES

Real Wages in Manufacturing
1890–1914

BY ALBERT REES
UNIVERSITY OF CHICAGO

assisted by Donald P. Jacobs

A STUDY BY THE
NATIONAL BUREAU OF ECONOMIC RESEARCH, NEW YORK

PUBLISHED BY
PRINCETON UNIVERSITY PRESS, PRINCETON
1961

v

RELATION OF THE DIRECTORS TO THE WORK AND PUBLICATIONS OF THE NATIONAL BUREAU OF ECONOMIC RESEARCH

1. The object of the National Bureau of Economic Research is to ascertain and to present to the public important economic facts and their interpretation in a scientific and impartial manner. The Board of Directors is charged with the responsibility of ensuring that the work of the National Bureau is carried on in strict conformity with this object.

2. To this end the Board of Directors shall appoint one or more Directors of Research.

3. The Director or Directors of Research shall submit to the members of the Board, or to its Executive Committee, for their formal adoption, all specific proposals concerning researches to be instituted.

4. No report shall be published until the Director or Directors of Research shall have submitted to the Board a summary drawing attention to the character of the data and their utilization in the report, the nature and treatment of the problems involved, the main conclusions, and such other information as in their opinion would serve to determine the suitability of the report for publication in accordance with the principles of the National Bureau.

5. A copy of any manuscript proposed for publication shall also be submitted to each member of the Board. For each manuscript to be so submitted a special committee shall be appointed by the President, or at his designation by the Executive Director, consisting of three Directors selected as nearly as may be one from each general division of the Board. The names of the special manuscript committee shall be stated to each Director when the summary and report described in paragraph (4) are sent to him. It shall be the duty of each member of the committee to read the manuscript. If each member of the special committee signifies his approval within thirty days, the manuscript may be published. If each member of the special committee has not signified his approval within thirty days of the transmittal of the report and manuscript, the Director of Research shall then notify each member of the Board, requesting approval or disapproval of publication, and thirty additional days shall be granted for this purpose. The manuscript shall then not be published unless at least a majority of the entire Board and a two-thirds majority of those members of the Board who shall have voted on the proposal within the time fixed for the receipt of votes on the publication proposed shall have approved.

6. No manuscript may be published, though approved by each member of the special committee, until forty-five days have elapsed from the transmittal of the summary and report. The interval is allowed for the receipt of any memorandum of dissent or reservation, together with a brief statement of his reasons, that any member may wish to express; and such memorandum of dissent or reservation shall be published with the manuscript if he so desires. Publication does not, however, imply that each member of the Board has read the manuscript, or that either members of the Board in general, or of the special committee, have passed upon its validity in every detail.

7. A copy of this resolution shall, unless otherwise determined by the Board, be printed in each copy of every National Bureau book.

(Resolution adopted October 25, 1926 and revised February 6, 1933 and February 24, 1941)

Contents

vii

Tables

Charts

xiii

Preface

THIS study was undertaken in 1954 as part of the National Bureau's study of trends in wages and productivity in the United States, a research program undertaken with the assistance of grants from the Alfred P. Sloan Foundation. The Foundation is, however, in no way responsible for the conclusions.

I should like to thank Leo Wolman for first suggesting this study to me; for his help, encouragement, and patience as the work progressed; and for making available his files and workbooks, on which we have drawn at several points.

Donald P. Jacobs participated actively in the research from its beginning almost to the end. He supervised much of the day-to-day work of gathering and processing data and has read and commented on the draft manuscript.

Robert E. Weintraub did a large part of the work of collecting and processing wage data. Joseph Guggenheim collected the data for the rent index and computed most of it. Sandra Gottlieb began the collection of data for the clothing and home furnishings price indexes. The index of illuminating gas prices is the work of Dan Moose, and much of the final computation of the cost-of-living index was done by Harry Gilman.

The clothing and home furnishings indexes were greatly improved by suggestions made by Dorothy S. Brady and Ethel D. Hoover. Margaret G. Reid gave valuable advice on the rent index and read and commented on the draft of Chapter 4.

During the last half of the study, H. Gregg Lewis was a constant adviser. He read the draft manuscript and made many helpful suggestions. Valuable comments on the draft manuscript were also proffered by Gerhard Bry, Daniel Creamer, Zvi Griliches, Harry McAllister, Clarence D. Long, and George Soule.

Firth Haring prepared the manuscript for press. H. Irving Forman drew the charts.

Our indebtedness to Paul H. Douglas will soon become obvious to any reader. Though we have frequent occasion to disagree with his estimates, they have constantly served as our point of departure.

We are grateful to Sears, Roebuck and Company and to Montgomery Ward & Company for their permission to use files of catalogues at their main offices. In particular, Edward Zink at Sears' and Fred W. Jameson at Ward's were of great assistance to us.

ALBERT REES

REAL WAGES IN MANUFACTURING
1890–1914

CHAPTER 1

Introduction and Summary

THE economic history of the United States has been marked by a strong and persistent rise in real wages. Only one period has seemed to stand out as an exception to this trend—the twenty-five years just before World War I. Previous students of this period have concluded that real wages from 1890 to 1914 were essentially stationary.

Such a long break in the upward trend of real wages could occur for one of two basic reasons. Perhaps the economy as a whole was stagnant during this period and per capita national income did not rise. What we know about changes in productivity and improvements in technology during the period seems to rule out this explanation. Or perhaps there were special factors affecting the labor market that prevented wage earners from sharing in the rise of per capita income.

The second explanation is more plausible than the first. The period 1890–1914 differs from earlier periods in that the frontier had closed by about 1890, in the sense that little good agricultural land was still available for original settlement. The period also differs from both earlier and later periods in the volume and composition of immigration. Many more immigrants came to the United States in this period than in any other of equal length, and more of them came from places where levels of skill and education were low. These forces could have worked to lower the incomes of wage earners relative to other incomes.

We undertook this study because the forces just mentioned did not seem to us to be powerful enough to account fully for the recorded behavior of the trend of real wages. We felt that part, at least, of this behavior might be the result of faulty statistics. This led us to construct new estimates of real wages for workers in manufacturing.

Our estimates of money wages differ from those available previously in having a broader coverage of manufacturing wage earners. They are based on data from the *Censuses of Manufactures* and the reports of the labor bureaus of several states. Our estimates of average hourly money earnings are shown in the first column of Table 1. These estimates lie at a lower level than the best estimates

3

TABLE 1

Average Hourly Earnings, All Manufacturing, 1890–1914
(money and real terms)

	Average Hourly Earnings (current dollars)	Cost-of-Living Index (1914 = 100)	Average Hourly Earnings[a] (1914 dollars)
1890	0.144	91	0.158
1891	0.144	91	0.158
1892	0.145	91	0.160
1893	0.151	90	0.168
1894	0.139	86	0.162
1895	0.138	84	0.165
1896	0.144	84	0.172
1897	0.140	83	0.168
1898	0.137	83	0.166
1899	0.146	83	0.176
1900	0.151	84	0.179
1901	0.158	85	0.185
1902	0.165	86	0.191
1903	0.170	88	0.193
1904	0.169	89	0.190
1905	0.172	88	0.194
1906	0.184	90	0.204
1907	0.191	94	0.203
1908	0.184	92	0.201
1909	0.186	91	0.203
1910	0.198	95	0.209
1911	0.202	95	0.213
1912	0.207	97	0.213
1913	0.221	99	0.224
1914	0.220	100	0.220

SOURCE: See Tables 10, 22, and 44, following.

a Here, and throughout the study, the figures shown have been rounded independently. Thus this last column was computed from data having more places than are shown in columns one and two.

previously available, those of Paul H. Douglas.[1] However, the trend of our estimates of money wages is only very slightly steeper than that of Douglas's estimates.

We have also constructed a new cost-of-living index for 1890–1914, shown in the second column of Table 1. This index uses Douglas's estimates of changes in the prices of food, liquor, and tobacco. It incorporates new indexes of the retail prices of clothing and home furnishings, based on mail order catalogues. These replace the

1 Presented in his pioneering study *Real Wages in the United States, 1890–1926*, Boston, 1930.

wholesale price indexes used by Douglas. We have also developed an index of rents based on newspaper advertisements. The inclusion of rents and the correspondingly lower weight given to food account for the largest part of the difference between the NBER cost-of-living index and the Douglas index. Finally, we have constructed a new index of prices for fuel and light, using more retail prices and fewer whole-sale prices than Douglas used. Rates for illuminating gas before 1907, which are the major new element in this fuel and light index, were obtained from utility companies.

Our index of the cost of living rises appreciably less than Douglas's. When we use it to deflate our money wage series, we find that the real earnings of manufacturing workers rose 37 per cent from 1890 to 1914, or at an annual compound rate of 1.3 per cent (see the last column of Table 1). This rate of increase is slightly lower than that shown for manufacturing by Clarence D. Long's study of changes in real wages from 1860 to 1890.[2] It is considerably lower than the rate of increase in real wages since 1914. These differences suggest that the closing of the frontier and the high level of immigration in our period did have some effect in holding down real wages, though not nearly as large an effect as previously believed.

The rate of growth of real wages in manufacturing for 1890–1914, as shown by our study, is less rapid than the increase in output per man-hour in manufacturing. This is to be expected because capital-output ratios in manufacturing were rising until 1919. The costs of using more capital per unit of output had to be covered before real wages could rise if the influx of capital was to be sustained. However, the rate of growth of real wages was the same as the rate of growth of output per weighted unit of labor and capital combined for the private domestic economy, as estimated by John W. Kendrick.[3]

Chapter 2 reviews the measures of changes in real wages presented in the previous literature and discusses the explanations advanced for the failure of real wages to rise. Chapter 3 presents our measures of money wages in all manufacturing and in several manufacturing industries, and explains the methods used to derive them. Chapter 4 discusses the construction of our cost-of-living index. Chapter 5 deals with the movement of our real wage series and returns to the dis-cussion of its relation to trends in productivity.

[2] *Wages and Earnings in the United States, 1860–1890*, Princeton University Press for National Bureau of Economic Research, 1960.

[3] *Productivity Trends in the United States*, Princeton University Press for National Bureau of Economic Research, in press.

CHAPTER 2

The Background for the Study

THE earliest estimates of real wages for any part of the period 1890–1914 can be found in Bulletin 53 of the Bureau of Labor.[1] This bulletin brought together the retail prices of food collected for the *Eighteenth Annual Report of the Commissioner of Labor*,[2] then in press, and the money wage series of the *Nineteenth Annual Report*,[3] then in preparation. These two sets of data were combined into two series of index numbers of "the purchasing power of wages measured by retail prices of food," which were maintained by regular collection of new data and published in subsequent bulletins[4] until 1907. The two indexes, one based on hourly wages and the other on full-time weekly wages (hourly wages times standard or full-time hours), are shown in the first column of Tables 2 and 3. The hourly index shows a small, irregular rise over the period; the weekly index has no appreciable trend. The money wage series used in constructing these indexes covered sixty-seven industries, not confined to manufacturing.[5] The wage statistics for each industry were simple averages of relatives for occupations, and the industries were combined using as weights the aggregate wage bill of each industry according to the Census of 1900. The index of retail food prices was an average of relatives for thirty food items weighted by expenditures on these items in 1901 for a subsample of 2,567 families. It was taken from Part I of the *Eighteenth Annual Report*.

After 1907 the regular work of the Bureau of Labor was interrupted for four years, apparently by the intensive inquiry then made into the conditions of labor of women and children. When the work was resumed by the Bureau of Labor Statistics (BLS) after 1911, it was

[1] July 1904, p. 723.
[2] *Cost of Living and Retail Prices of Food*, 1904.
[3] *Wages and Hours of Labor*, 1905.
[4] Nos. 59, 65, 71, and 77.
[5] The nonmanufacturing industries (as defined in the *Census of Manufactures, 1905*) were blacksmithing and horseshoeing; building trades; men's custom work; and streets and sewers, municipal work. In addition, two industries were included that were then considered part of manufacturing and are not now: illuminating and heating gas, and steam railroad cars (now excluded if built by railroad companies).

6

TABLE 2

Five Indexes of Real Hourly Wages, 1890–1914[a]

(1890–99 = 100)

	Bulletin 77	Rubinow	Jones	Douglas and Lamberson	Douglas, All Manufacturing
1890	97.9	98.3	97.9	97.5	95
1891	96.6	96.6	96.2	96.0	98
1892	98.9	98.7	98.4	98.5	98
1893	96.6	97.2	96.9	97.1	101
1894	98.2	99.7	99.2	98.8	102
1895	100.5	101.5	100.8	101.1	101
1896	104.4	105.0	104.7	105.3	102
1897	103.4	103.0	103.4	103.6	100
1898	101.5	100.5	101.5	101.2	100
1899	102.5	100.6	101.9	101.6	101
1900	104.4	101.6	103.6	103.7	101
1901	102.7	98.6	101.7	100.1	100
1902	101.2	97.7	101.0	98.5	101
1903	105.4	100.7	104.7	102.2	100
1904	104.7	100.0	104.1	101.7	101
1905	105.8	102.8	106.4	103.1	103
1906	107.3	102.7	106.8	103.9	103
1907	106.8	102.7	107.2	104.2	101
1908	—	98.8	103.0	101.2	102
1909	—	94.7	98.5	97.2	102
1910	—	93.0	96.5	95.1	100
1911	—	95.3	99.0	97.8	98
1912	—	91.8	95.0	94.6	102
1913	—	—	—	96.1	102
1914	—	—	—	96.5	102

[a] All series except Douglas's show the purchasing power of wages in terms of food only. For sources and methods, see text.

much changed. The number of food items whose prices were collected dropped from thirty to fifteen. The amount of wage data collected within each industry was increased, but the number of industries covered decreased sharply. For some industries, union rates were collected, rather than rates taken from employer payrolls. Most of the new series ran back through the missing years 1907–11, but no official average has ever been published of the new wage series for 1907–14, nor, of course, any official continuation of the series on the purchasing power of wages in terms of food.

7

TABLE 3

Six Indexes of Real Full-Time Weekly Wages, 1890–1914[a]

(1890–99 = 100)

	Bulletin 77	Rubinow	Jones	Douglas and Lamberson	Hansen[b]	Douglas, All Manufacturing
1890	98.6	99.4	98.9	98.4	94	96
1891	97.1	97.5	97.1	96.8	95	99
1892	99.4	99.4	99.1	99.3	98	99
1893	96.9	97.6	97.3	97.5	97	101
1894	98.0	98.9	98.4	98.7	99	101
1895	100.6	102.2	101.4	101.2	101	102
1896	104.2	104.7	104.4	104.6	104	101
1897	103.0	102.5	102.9	103.2	107	100
1898	101.2	100.1	101.1	100.5	104	100
1899	101.7	99.8	101.1	100.3	101	100
1900	103.0	100.2	102.1	101.6	99	100
1901	100.7	96.8	99.8	97.6	101	99
1902	98.5	94.3	98.4	95.1	101	99
1903	101.8	97.3	101.3	97.6	100	98
1904	100.4	96.0	99.9	96.9	100	98
1905	101.4	98.6	102.1	98.3	102	100
1906	102.4	98.0	101.9	98.6	101	99
1907	101.5	97.7	102.0	98.2	100	97
1908	—	93.0	97.3	94.6	102	97
1909	—	89.4	92.9	90.7	99	98
1910	—	87.2	90.6	87.8	98	95
1911	—	88.9	92.4	90.1	100	93
1912	—	85.3	88.4	85.9	100	96
1913	—	—	—	86.8	98	95
1914	—	—	—	87.0	98	95

[a] All of these indexes except the last two show the purchasing power of wages in terms of food only. For sources and methods, see text.

[b] Converted from the original base 1913 = 100.

In 1914, I. M. Rubinow published the first index of real wages covering the period after 1907.[6] His money wage series covered the building trades and fourteen manufacturing industries for which continuous data were available since 1890. (No use was made of the data available, up to 1907, for other industries.) After 1907 the data underlying the series for the building trades and five other

[6] "The Recent Trend of Real Wages," *American Economic Review*, December 1914, pp. 793–817.

8

series[7] were union rates; the data underlying the nine remaining series[8] were from payrolls. For all the payroll industries except carbuilding, the indexes used were computed by the Bureau of Labor Statistics and were employment-weighted averages of occupational relatives. For carbuilding and the union-rate industries, Rubinow computed simple averages of relatives. The fifteen industries were combined in a simple average. On the price side, Rubinow used a weighted index, computed by the Bureau, including only the fifteen food items whose prices had been collected continuously since 1890.

Rubinow's results, which indicate a sharp fall in real wages after 1907, are shown in the second column of Tables 2 and 3. His estimates are based throughout on the continuous series only. They differ, therefore, from those of Bulletin 77 even prior to 1907. Rubinow states his conclusions as follows: "When confronted with a rapidly rising price movement (accompanied as it was by a violent growth of profits), the American wage-worker, notwithstanding his strenuous efforts to adjust wages to these new price conditions, notwithstanding all the picturesque I.W.W.-ism, new unionism, and the modish sabotage, has been losing surely and not even slowly, so that the sum total of economic progress of this country for the last quarter of a century appears to be a loss of from 10 to 15 per cent in his earning power." [9]

In 1917, F. W. Jones published an amended version of Rubinow's results.[10] The sole change consisted of linking the price index of fifteen food items to the older series of thirty items at 1907, rather than using the fifteen items throughout. Jones' series are shown in the third column of Tables 2 and 3. Although they fall somewhat less than Rubinow's, they do not materially alter his conclusions. Indeed, Jones writes, "The doctrine so popular in certain quarters that while the rich have grown rapidly richer in recent years the poor have also steadily risen in the scale of economic welfare, has no foundation in fact." [11]

In 1921, Paul H. Douglas and Frances Lamberson published an article bringing Rubinow's series down to 1918.[12] Rejecting Jones's

---

[7] Bakers, marble and stone cutters, foundry and machine shops, book and job printing, and newspaper printing.

[8] Cotton goods, woolen goods, silk goods, boots and shoes, knit goods, lumber, millwork, furniture, and carbuilding.

[9] "Trend of Real Wages," p. 812.

[10] "Real Wages in Recent Years," *American Economic Review*, June 1917, pp. 317–330.

[11] *Ibid.*, p. 330.

[12] "The Movement of Real Wages, 1890–1918," *American Economic Review*, September 1921, pp. 409–426.

improvement, they returned to the index of fifteen food items. On the wage side, they found that continuous data were available until 1918 for only ten of Rubinow's fifteen industries, of which only three had payroll data.[13] New indexes were computed for these ten industries for 1912–18, based on simple averages of occupational relatives, and these were spliced to Rubinow's series at 1912. The final wage indexes were simple averages of the ten industry indexes. Since only ten industries were used even prior to 1912, the results differ slightly from Rubinow's before that date. These results are shown in the fourth column of Tables 2 and 3. They show a slight rise of real earnings from 1912 to 1914, but not nearly enough to offset the fall from 1907 to 1912.

In 1925 Alvin H. Hansen made another computation of real wages for this period.[14] He accepted the full-time weekly money wage series of Douglas and Lamberson, but computed a new cost-of-living index. This included the BLS index of the retail price of food (based on thirty items to 1907 and fifteen items thereafter) with a weight of 40; and the BLS wholesale price indexes of cloths and clothing (weight 17), fuel and light (weight 6), and house furnishings (weight 5). The weights are approximations of the pattern of family expenditures shown by the 1918 budget study of the Bureau of Labor Statistics.[15] Thus, for the first time, the purchasing power of wages during this period was not expressed entirely in terms of food.

Hansen's index is shown in the fifth column of Table 3. It shows no trend; although 1914 lies slightly above 1890, it lies slightly below the average for 1890–99. This flatness implies an increase in real hourly earnings, for which Hansen made no index. Hansen comments on the fall in real wages from the peak reached by his index in 1897, explaining it as a result of a lag of wages behind prices during an inflation. He states, in part: "Rising prices amount in fact to a redistribution of the national income in favor of the entrepreneurial class. It amounts to an enforced taxation of wage-earners, salaried persons, investors and landlords with long-term rent contracts. In the period from 1897 to 1915 when real wages were falling in spite of an enormous increase in national production, business profits far outran

[13] The omitted industries are silk goods, knit goods, lumber, furniture, and car-building. In addition, only union rate data were now available for millwork, for which Rubinow had used payroll data.
[14] "Factors Affecting the Trend of Real Wages," *American Economic Review*, March 1925, pp. 25–42 and 294.
[15] *Cost of Living in the United States*, BLS Bulletin No. 357, May 1924.

10

the general price level."[16] Elsewhere he adds, "Undoubtedly the lag of real wages behind production from 1897 to 1915 was to some extent the result of the increasing scarcity of land."[17]

It was against this background that Douglas's book[18] appeared. Of course, *Real Wages* covers far more than manufacturing. We shall be concerned here with its manufacturing series only. It is one of the virtues of this work that, for the first time, it separated wages in manufacturing from wages in the building trades and presented manufacturing wages alone. The number of manufacturing industries covered was increased to fourteen by interpolation in some of the series containing gaps. Six of the series were based on union rates[19] and eight on payroll data.[20] Within industries, the averages were weighted averages of actual rates (rather than of relatives); the industries were combined using census employment weights.

For the cost-of-living estimates, Douglas followed Hansen in using wholesale prices where retail prices were not available. The former were used for clothing, furniture, and spirits and tobacco, and for fuel and light until 1907. The retail prices of gas and coal, collected by the BLS since 1907, were used for 1907–14. The food index used twenty-nine items at retail until 1907 and fifteen thereafter. The fourteen omitted items were continued by means of wholesale prices until 1914 and throughout the period for eleven items for which retail prices had not been collected before 1907. All wholesale prices (both of foods and nonfoods) were adjusted to a presumed retail basis according to the differences between the wholesale and retail price indexes of identical food items. The various group indexes were combined using family expenditure weights for 1901 from the *Eighteenth Annual Report*.

Douglas's results are shown in the last column of Tables 2 and 3.

---

[16] Hansen, "Factors Affecting Real Wages," p. 40. Several economic historians, including Wesley C. Mitchell and Earl J. Hamilton, have noted lags of wages behind prices in inflations of the nineteenth century and earlier. Like Hansen, they argued that this increased profits. However, inflations in the United States since 1914 have clearly been accompanied by rising real wages. It is not clear whether this difference represents a change in the behavior of wages in recent inflations or whether it represents an improvement in the quality of the data on which the wage and price series are based. Hansen's use of weekly earnings deflated by consumers' prices is inappropriate for drawing inferences about profits. Hourly earnings deflated by the prices of the products produced would be more appropriate.

[17] *Ibid.*, p. 36.

[18] *Real Wages in the United States, 1890–1926*, Boston, 1930.

[19] Metal trades, granite and stone, book and job printing, newspaper printing, planing mills, and bakers.

[20] Cotton, boots and shoes, clothing, hosiery and knit goods, woolens, lumber, iron and steel, and slaughtering and meat packing.

11

The real hourly earnings series shows a slight rise over the whole period covered, for the first time since Bulletin 77. However, much of the rise occurs in the single year 1890–91, and all of it by 1894. In 1914 the series on real weekly earnings lies slightly further below its 1890–99 average than does Hansen's.

After the appearance of Douglas's book, discussion of the course of real wages before 1914 came to a halt. Perhaps this was because Douglas had made most of the possible refinements in processing the BLS data. Perhaps, since his series showed some slight rise in real hourly earnings, there no longer seemed to be any problem to solve. Perhaps, too, as time passed there was less interest in the period before World War I.

Nevertheless, the passing of time heightens the uneasiness that one feels on reviewing Douglas's results. We have become accustomed to the idea that continuously improving technology, the accumulation of physical capital, and rising levels of education have combined to bring steady, substantial improvement in the standard of living of all major groups in our population.[21] Was the material progress of manufacturing workers really interrupted for almost a quarter of a century? If so, why?

A second puzzle may also be considered. Douglas estimates that real full-time weekly earnings in manufacturing fell about 1 per cent from 1890 to 1914, and 5 per cent from the decade average 1890–99 to 1914. He also estimates that this fall in real weekly earnings was accompanied by a reduction in full-time weekly hours from 60.0 in 1890 to 55.2 in 1914. The historical record for longer periods suggests that an increase in real hourly earnings will be used in part to increase real earnings exclusive of leisure (to increase the consumption of goods and services) and in part to reduce hours of work (to increase the consumption of leisure). This record is entirely consistent with a theory of the demand for leisure in which it is a normal commodity for which the demand is relatively stable over time.[22] But the record as a whole does not suggest that leisure is so strongly preferred that workers will consume all of an increase in hourly earnings in the form of leisure and will, in addition, cut into their previous consumption of goods and services to shorten hours. Douglas's findings suggest a

---

[21] For an eloquent statement of this view, see Solomon Fabricant, *Economic Progress and Economic Change*, Thirty-fourth Annual Report, National Bureau of Economic Research, New York, 1954.

[22] See H. G. Lewis, "Hours of Work and Hours of Leisure," *Proceedings of the Ninth Annual Meeting of the Industrial Relations Research Association*, 1957, pp. 196–206.

strong unexplained shift of preferences toward leisure during this period (unless it is assumed that shorter hours were forced on unwilling workers by employers, governments, or unions, which seems most unlikely). Putting the matter differently, we can say that Douglas's results might be easier to accept if they showed hourly earnings, weekly hours, and weekly earnings all unchanged, implying a complete absence of progress. As they now stand they show modest progress used entirely to shorten the workweek, and still failing to account for all the shortening that occurred.

In the writings of Rubinow and Hansen we have already encountered one explanation for the failure of real wages to rise. They stated that wages lagged behind prices, resulting in abnormally high profits. Our willingness to accept this explanation must be tempered by the experience of more recent periods of rising prices. Douglas shows a rise of 11 per cent in real hourly earnings in manufacturing from 1914 to 1920, a period in which the cost of living more than doubled. More recently, real average hourly earnings in manufacturing have increased 62 per cent from 1939 to 1957, a period in which the Consumer Price Index doubled.

Another possible cause of the failure of real wages to rise in this period is the closing of the frontier. For earlier periods it has been argued that the existence of free or cheap land in the West served as a "safety valve" for labor. It absorbed part of the inflow of immigrants, and part of the natural increase of population in the rural East that might otherwise have gone into urban employment. Perhaps there was also some direct movement of eastern urban workers to the frontier, though they were more likely to become workers in frontier towns than farmers.

By 1900, however, the pull of the frontier must have been greatly weakened. A distinguished economic historian writes: "By the close of the century the supply of free and fertile farming land had almost disappeared."[23]

After about 1898, the rate of growth of agricultural output decreased sharply. In the sixteen years from 1898 to 1914, agricultural output increased 22 per cent; in the preceding sixteen years, it had increased 46 per cent.[24] Urban population continued to grow

[23] Chester W. Wright, *Economic History of the United States*, 2nd ed., New York, 1949, p. 462.
[24] Frederick Strauss and Louis H. Bean, *Gross Farm Income and Indices of Farm Production and Prices in the United States, 1869–1937*, U.S. Department of Agriculture Technical Bulletin No. 703, Table 58.

13

rapidly. The combination of rapid urban growth with slackened agricultural growth helped to bring about the rise in the price of farm products that began in 1896 and thus helped to limit the gains in urban real wages.[25]

Douglas is more concerned with explaining the rise in real wages over the whole period 1890–1926 than with explaining their failure to rise until 1914. However, in his discussion, he introduces one major factor, immigration, that clearly operated differently in the two parts of his period. If, as Douglas believes, the curtailment of immigration during and after the war caused real wages to rise, the unprecedented level of immigration just before the war and the low levels of skill and literacy of the immigrants may well have had an opposite effect.[26] This argument is put directly by W. I. King, who estimated from census data that real annual earnings (money annual earnings deflated by the wholesale price index) declined slightly from 1900 to 1910. He explained his finding in what may well be one of the purplest passages in the literature of academic economics:

"And so, the dawn of the twentieth century saw the spoilers gazing longingly from east and west at the riches wrested by American brawn and brains from the grasp of Nature. The advance guard of the Asiatics reached our Pacific coast but the forces of labor organized against the "Yellow Peril" and successfully repelled the invasion. But into our Atlantic ports, unresisted and almost unheeded, pounced, at the same time, another army of invaders, the "White Peril" from Southern and Eastern Europe. And still it comes! Its advance is marked by no waving banners, no rattle of musketry, and no boom of artillery, but the army streams in company by company, regiment by regiment, brigade by brigade and division by division. . . . The low standard of the Old World tends to force itself upon the New and turn back the tide of progress."[27]

This explanation, if soberly stated, is not unreasonable. A great influx of unskilled labor could both drive down money wages and bid up the prices of those commodities consumed primarily by the lowest

---

[25] We are indebted to George Soule for pointing out the importance of changes in agricultural output in this context.

[26] For annual estimates of net immigration during this period, see Simon Kuznets and Ernest Rubin, *Immigration and the Foreign Born*, Occasional Paper 46, New York, NBER, 1954.

[27] Willford Isbell King, *The Wealth and Income of the People of the United States*, New York, 1919, pp. 175–177.

14

income groups. The real wages of all workers, including the immigrants, would tend to fall.[28]

Before we accept this explanation, however, we should note that in roughly the same period we are considering available estimates of real wages for other countries also fail to rise or rise slowly, and these countries did not have net immigration. The most dramatic case is the United Kingdom, where Phelps Brown and Hopkins find that real hourly wages were unchanged from 1890 to 1913.[29] These authors also report a retardation in the increase of real wages after 1886 in three of the four other countries studied, the United States, France, and Germany.[30] This retardation is called "the late nineteenth-century climacteric." On the basis of their work on real income per capita, the authors comment on the change in the movement of real wages: "One hypothesis can be put aside at the outset: this change does not seem to have arisen from a change adverse to labour in the distribution of the national income."[31] Thus they disagree with the basic position of Rubinow and Hansen. Instead they believe that the "climacteric" resulted from a "check to productivity" and that this in turn came about because progress in technology had turned toward new products and away from new processes for making old products at lower cost.

In so far as this explanation applies to the United States, let us examine it in the light of productivity data. John W. Kendrick has recently estimated that total factor productivity (output per unit of all tangible inputs) in the private domestic economy rose at an average annual rate of 1.3 per cent a year from 1889 to 1919, and that, over the same period, the output-labor ratio rose 1.6 per cent annually.[32] For manufacturing, Fabricant finds a decrease of 27 per cent in man-hours per unit of output from 1899 to 1914.[33] These rates are substantially below the corresponding rates for more recent periods,

28 However, the real wages of those already on the scene when the immigration began might tend to rise. The original labor force can, for the most part, be regarded as a factor (skilled or semiskilled labor) whose real returns rise because of an increased supply of a complementary factor (unskilled labor).

29 E. H. Phelps Brown with Sheila V. Hopkins, "The Course of Wage-Rates in Five Countries, 1860–1939," *Oxford Economic Papers*, n.s. II, 1950, pp. 226–296. The real wage series for the United Kingdom is based largely on the work of G. H. Wood and A. L. Bowley.

30 The exception is Sweden. The United States data used for 1890–1913 are from Douglas, *Real Wages*.

31 Phelps Brown and Hopkins, "Course of Wage-Rates," p. 238.

32 Thirty-eighth Annual Report, New York, NBER, 1958, p. 61.

33 Solomon Fabricant, *Employment in Manufacturing, 1899–1939*, New York, NBER, 1942, p. 331.

but they are far above the rates of growth of real wages shown by Douglas. The 27 per cent fall in the labor-output ratio for manufacturing may be compared with a rise of 1 per cent in real hourly earnings for the same years. The average annual percentage rate of growth in real wages shown by Douglas for 1890–1919 is 0.4 per cent, compared with the growth rates for productivity of 1.3 and 1.6 per cent in Kendrick's estimates. It should be noted that this rise in average productivity took place despite the immigration of the unskilled, which should by itself tend to reduce average productivity as well as real wages.

Whatever the correspondence of estimates of productivity and real wages for other countries, those for the United States clearly diverge. It is possible, of course, that real wages were held down by immigration in the United States at precisely the same time as they were held down by the lag of productivity in the United Kingdom. However, the correspondence in timing suggests the possibility of some common cause, either real or arising from the kinds of data collected and the statistical procedures used for that period.

There is an especially strong possibility that the similarities of movement of real wages in the United States and the United Kingdom arise in part from similar kinds of errors in measuring the cost of living. In both cases, the official, complete cost-of-living indexes begin in 1914, and, in both cases, the indexes before that date are put together from inadequate or fragmentary materials. In Britain, as in the United States, retail prices were collected before 1914 only for a few items of food and fuel, and wholesale prices had to be used to estimate several components of the cost of living.[34]

When, in the exploratory phase of this study, we reviewed the reasons advanced in the literature for the failure of real wages to rise appreciably during the period, we were dissatisfied. None of them seemed compelling enough to rule out the possibility that all the writers we have cited were seeking to explain something that never happened. The course of our own work has since made even clearer to us the temptation to economic statisticians to rationalize in terms of real forces results that eventually prove to arise from statistical error. And major sources of possible error seemed to be present in all the estimates of real wages in the United States before World War I. On the money wage side, there was the heavy reliance on union rates

[34] For a description of the British data, see A. L. Bowley, *Wages and Income in the United Kingdom Since 1860*, Cambridge, 1937, Appendix D.

in a period when unions were relatively unimportant. On the price side, there was the almost complete reliance on wholesale prices for nonfoods, and the absence of any series for rents.

It did not seem possible to improve on Douglas's processing of the materials he used. We therefore decided to construct new estimates using new sources of data as far as possible. The problem that gave rise to the study was one of long-term trends, and this has guided our acceptance or rejection of data. Although our work may have some value for cyclical problems, it must be used for such problems with great caution, for, at times, our data or our procedures would be inadequate or inappropriate for an investigation of cyclical fluctuation.

CHAPTER 3

Money Wages

THIS chapter is concerned with the movement of money wages in manufacturing and the discussion is restricted to wage earners or production workers. Data are available on the annual earnings of salaried workers, but we have not made use of them. Figures on hourly earnings are not available.

Although we have spoken of "wages" above and will do so throughout the chapter, this expression is used for brevity and is not strictly accurate. We are measuring changes in average hourly earnings, defined as total wage-earner payrolls divided by the number of man-hours worked. These differ from wage rates, which are the basic hourly rates for specific tasks established by employers or by unions. Our measures of average hourly earnings are affected throughout by shifts in the occupational and industrial composition of the work force, as well as by changes in wage rates for particular occupations. An index of wage rates with constant weights would not reflect such shifts in composition. At the end of this chapter we report one test in which we hold industry weights constant and find that this makes no difference in the movement of our series.

Other sources of difference between wage rates and average hourly earnings, such as overtime and shift premiums, are important today but were probably not so during the period of our study. Payment by piece rates, however, was important. For workers paid on piece rates rather than time rates, average hourly earnings will rise as output per man-hour rises even if the piece rates are constant.

A study of wage movements for a more recent period would also have to take account of wage supplements or fringe benefits. We have no data on wage supplements during the period but believe them to be negligible. Toward the end of the period, employers' premiums for workmen's compensation would have been present in some states.[1]

[1] Our data may also fail to catch some wages paid in kind. The instructions for the Census of 1905 state that room and board furnished as part payment of wages are to be included in wages, but this instruction may not always have been followed (see *Census of Manufactures, 1905*, Part I, p. 578).

The next section of this chapter deals with the sources and methods used by Douglas in his estimates of money wages. The following sections discuss our own sources and methods, and present our estimates of money wages for all manufacturing and for a number of individual manufacturing industries. Wherever possible, we make comparisons between our estimates and data from independent sources and seek to explain the differences that are found.

We find that Douglas's estimates of money wages for all manufacturing and for a number of industries are at too high a level because of his reliance on union rates. However, the differences in trend are minor.

Douglas's Data

Those of the studies discussed in Chapter 2 that run beyond 1907 use two kinds of money-wage data: union rates and occupational earnings taken from payrolls. A discussion of the limitations of these data will make clearer our reasons for turning to alternative sources.

Union rates have two kinds of defects. First, they tend to be more stable through time than the earnings actually received by union members. Second, when used to represent industries only partially unionized, their absolute level is too high. Both of these defects were recognized by Leo Wolman as early as 1932,[2] but no alternative series is available that remedies them.

On the first point Wolman wrote: "Union wage rates, moreover, have defects peculiar to themselves. They rarely reflect actual changes in the rate of wages and, particularly during periods of depression they can be regarded as no more than nominal rates which conceal the true movement of wages. This is indubitably the case with the reported union rates of wages during the present depression in the building and other unionized industries, with the possible exception of the printing industry. That the same policy of reporting nominal data has been observed in earlier depressions is, I think, beyond question."[3]

To show the effects of the use of union rates to describe the level of wages for the whole of partially unionized industries, Wolman

---

[2] "American Wages," *Quarterly Journal of Economics*, February 1932, pp. 398–406. This is a review note of Douglas's *Real Wages in the United States, 1890–1926*. For a more recent criticism along the same lines, see "Nongovernmental Historical Series on Earnings, Wages, and Hours," *Monthly Labor Review*, August 1955, pp. 918–919, a technical note based on a memorandum by Witt Bowden.

[3] "American Wages," pp. 401–402.

compared Douglas's union rate data with payroll data from the National Industrial Conference Board (NICB). These comparisons for 1914 are shown in Table 4; we have added "foundries and machine shops" to the industries shown by Wolman.

TABLE 4

Union Rates and Payroll Data, Three Industries, 1914
(cents per hour)

	Union Rates (Douglas)[a]	Hourly Earnings (NICB)[b]
Book and job printing	45.1	30.2
Newspaper printing	61.0	37.8
Planing mills[c]	40.4	22.4
Foundries and machine shops[d]	41.3	27.8

[a] Paul H. Douglas, *Real Wages in the Unites States, 1890–1926*, Boston, 1930, p. 96.

[b] National Industrial Conference Board, *Wages and Hours in American Industry*, New York, 1925, pp. 176, 180, 188, and 124; data are for July. See also Leo Wolman, *The Growth of American Trade Unions, 1880–1923*, New York, NBER, 1924, p. 402.

[c] Called "lumber manufacturing and mill work" by NICB, but excludes sawmills.

[d] The union rate data are for "metal trades." They include quotations from industries other than foundries and machine shops, but Douglas gives them the census weight of that industry. For further details see pp. 59–60.

Although none of Douglas's series is based on union rates before 1907, errors of level affect the entire period from 1890, since the earlier data are linked to the later to provide continuity. (The high level of the union-rate data does not constitute evidence that unions raised wages—see p. 59–60 below.)

The problems involved in Douglas's use of union rates can also be seen by comparing the percentage of manufacturing workers organized with the portion of the total weight of Douglas's all-manufacturing series given to union rates. The union rates are clearly overweighted as a result of Douglas's decision in combining industries to weight union rates by the total number of skilled and semi-skilled workers in the industry rather than by union membership. Wolman has estimated the extent of union organization by industry in 1910. For the industries including the groups covered by the union-rate series, Wolman gives the following estimates of the percentage of union membership: metal trades, except iron and steel, 6.5 per cent; marble and stone yards, 45.4; bakeries, 17.4; printing

and publishing, 34.3; and lumber and furniture, 10.3.[4] For all manufacturing Wolman estimates the percentage organized in 1910 as
11.6, while Douglas gives to union rates 31.5 per cent of the total
weight of all manufacturing in 1910.[5]

The data for the payroll industries are far superior to those for
union industries. Nevertheless, they too present problems. The most
important of these is that prior to 1914, data were collected only for
"selected occupations," generally those peculiar to the industry.
Thus, most of the unskilled workers, and perhaps some of the semi-
skilled, were excluded. Douglas deals with this difficulty by linking
the data for specified occupations to those for all occupations at 1914,
thus accepting the level of the 1914 data throughout the earlier part
of his series. This is clearly the best method available, and the results
seem to be satisfactory in most cases. The absence of data for the
unskilled may, nevertheless, be a source of error at some points.

A second difficulty is that in two of the payroll industries, Douglas
interpolated hourly earnings for part of the period by assuming that
they moved with annual earnings. The interpolations are for 1908–10
in clothing and for 1908–17 in meat packing. We have been unable
to make better estimates for either of these industries from alternative data. However, to the extent that Douglas's all-manufacturing
series rests on these interpolated data, it is subject to errors that can,
in part, be avoided.

The payroll data for basic iron and steel have a special defect; they
cover only certain departments of the industry. We will show later
that the omissions result in errors both of level and of movement.

The final reason for seeking alternatives to the payroll data is the
size and nature of the payroll sample. This sample is very small in the
early years of the period and clearly not a random one. The most
important discernable way in which it is nonrandom is in the size
of establishments included, which tend to be substantially larger than
the average of all establishments. Table 5 shows the changes in
sample size for three of the payroll industries, in absolute numbers
and as a percentage of census employment. The average number of
workers per establishment in the BLS sample in 1914 was 623 for
boots and shoes, 893 for cotton goods, and 835 for woolens and

---

[4] Leo Wolman, *The Growth of American Trade Unions, 1880–1923*, New York, 1924,
Appendix Table VII.
[5] Interpolated from the figures for 1904 and 1914 given in Douglas, *Real Wages*,
p. 94. Wolman, in "American Wages," makes a comparison for 1920 similar to that
made here for 1910.

21

TABLE 5

Coverage of BLS Payroll Samples, Three Industries, Census Years, 1890–1914

	BOOTS AND SHOES				COTTON GOODS				WOOLEN AND WORSTED			
	Establishments		Number of Workers[b]	% of Census Employment	Establishments		Number of Workers[b]	% of Census Employment	Establishments		Number of Workers[b]	% of Census Employment
	Number in Sample[a]	% of Census			Number in Sample[a]	% of Census			Number in Sample[a]	% of Census		
1890[c,d]	26	1.2	938	0.7	22	2.4[e]	6,498	3.0[e]	15	1.0	3,078	2.6
1899[d]	37	2.3	1,416	1.0	24	2.5	7,506	2.5	15	1.2	3,041	2.4
1904[f]	45	3.4	4,865	3.2	29	2.7	15,115	4.9	27	2.7	6,592	4.6
1909	26	1.9	4,090	2.2	36	3.0	12,698	3.4	19	2.1	6,798	4.2
1914[f]	84	6.2	51,054	26.6	90	7.6	78,582	20.7	48	6.0	40,061	25.2

SOURCE: *Nineteenth Annual Report of the Commissioner of Labor* (1905) and BLS Bulletins Nos. 232, 238, and 239.

[a] Number of establishments is shown in the sources for 1890, 1899, and 1904 by occupation only. The number shown here is the largest for any one occupation in the given year. The total for all occupations may exceed this number if some establishments did not report for the occupation shown here.

[b] The employment totals were computed under the direction of Leo Wolman and are taken from his workbooks in the files of the National Bureau of Economic Research.

[c] Census data shown for 1890 refer primarily to 1889.

[d] Census data exclude custom work and repairing.

[e] Census data include cotton smallwares.

[f] Two samples for the same year were taken in 1904 and in 1914, one comparable with the preceding year and one with the following year. The figures shown here refer to the larger of the two samples for each statistic separately.

worsteds. The corresponding averages from the Census of 1914 were 141, 323, and 199. Such comparisons are not possible for earlier years, when the BLS data do not include all the workers in each establishment. Presumably the disparities were larger when the BLS sample was much smaller.

These defects of the payroll data led us to make alternative estimates, wherever possible, for the payroll industries as well as for the union industries. However, as we will show, these alternative estimates for the payroll industries differ very little from Douglas's in most cases. In other words, the defects of the payroll data, though they seemed to be serious a priori, turned out to be surprisingly unimportant in practice.

Our Data and Methods

The purpose of this section is to give a very brief overview of our methods and sources, which we will explain in more detail as we proceed, and to relate our general methods to those of other investigators.[6]

Our basic method is to compute average annual earnings per full-time equivalent worker from the *Census of Manufactures* for census years. We then interpolate for intercensal years, using data from the reports of state labor bureaus to get a continuous series on annual earnings. These are then converted into daily earnings by use of the state data on the average number of days per year that establishments were in operation.[7] Finally the daily earnings are converted into hourly earnings by means of data on full-time hours from the *Census of Manufactures* for 1914 and 1909 and from the BLS bulletins previously discussed. This method was used to get an all-manufacturing series and separate series for fourteen manufacturing industries.

The method whose rough outlines we have just sketched is essentially identical with the method used by Douglas to derive hourly earnings for coal mining; he got the average number of days mines were in operation from the U.S. Geological Survey.[8] (The method used by Brissenden is like ours in that his estimates of hourly earnings

---

[6] In our first attempt to find new data on wages before 1914, we wrote to a large number of trade associations that have been in continuous existence since before 1914, asking them for any wage data preserved in their files. This effort was a complete failure; what little information we received was too scattered to be useful.

[7] In practice, we usually perform our interpolations with daily rather than annual earnings, but in a way that is equivalent to that described in the text.

[8] Douglas, *Real Wages*, pp. 142–165.

23

are ultimately based on census annual earnings, but the two methods are dissimilar in many other ways.[9]) So far as we know, no one has previously used the state establishment data on the average number of days in operation per year to reduce annual earnings in manufacturing to daily earnings.

The annual earnings estimates from which we start are very similar to those made by Douglas in Part III of *Real Wages*. But Douglas made no attempt to reconcile his annual earnings estimates in Part III with his estimates of full-time weekly earnings and hourly earnings in Part II. The discrepancies between Douglas's two sets of estimates were one of the things that led us to our own method.

The differences between Douglas's annual earnings series and his full-time weekly earnings series multiplied by 52 seem, in many cases, too large to be explained by the conceptual differences between the two measures. The two sets of data are shown in Table 6 for 1914 for all the industries where the comparison is possible. In every industry except slaughtering and meat packing, full-time weekly earnings times 52 exceed average annual earnings. In most industries the difference s large, and in the union industries, as we would expect, it is extremely large.

The state establishment data on days in operation permit us to get consistent annual and hourly earnings estimates. This means, in effect, that we accept the annual earnings estimates, and reject the kinds of hourly earnings estimates that have been built up from occupational data. One reason for doing this is that the coverage of the annual earnings data and the data on days in operation is very much broader. A second reason is that the method permits us to estimate hourly earnings for some industries for which no estimates have previously been available.

The breadth of coverage of the state data we used is illustrated in Table 7, which shows the same three industries (somewhat more broadly defined) for which payroll data coverage is shown in Table 5. These industries are among those for which both sets of data are the best, in the case of the state data because employment in these

9 Paul F. Brissenden, *Earnings of Factory Workers, 1899–1927*, Census Monograph X, Washington, 1929. Brissenden's method is extremely and needlessly complicated and no attempt will be made to summarize it here. Those interested in understanding it should see Brissenden's own description of it and Douglas's criticism in *Real Wages*, Appendix A. Brissenden's estimates rest heavily on some data of dubious reliability or representativeness, including, for example, the percentage of trade unionists in New York State unemployed in 1904.

industries was highly concentrated in states that published earnings statistics. A detailed discussion of the nature and quality of the state statistics we used may be found in Appendix A. A complete table of the coverage of the state data used is given in Appendix C.

TABLE 6

Comparisons Between Average Annual Earnings and Full-Time Weekly Earnings Times 52 (Douglas), 1914
(dollars)

Industry[a]	Average Annual Earnings	Full-Time Weekly Earnings × 52
Union Industries		
Foundries and machine shops[b]	674	1,065
Marble and stone	692	1,243
Book and job printing	693	1,123
Newspaper and periodical printing	774	1,424
Lumber planing mills	644	1,021
Bread and other bakery products	620	934
Payroll Industries		
Cotton goods	387	452
Boots and shoes	552	691
Men's clothing	500	683
Hosiery and knit goods	397	490
Woolen and worsted goods	479	521
Lumber and timber	500	622
Iron and steel works and rolling mills	758	1,015
Slaughtering and meat packing	629	627
All Manufacturing	580	824

SOURCE: Paul H. Douglas, *Real Wages in the United States, 1890–1926*, Boston, 1930.
[a] The industry names given are those of the annual earnings data; the order is that of the full-time weekly earnings data. The names of the corresponding full-time weekly earnings series (in order) are: metal trades, granite and stone, book and job printing, newspaper printing, planing mills, and bakers (for the union industries); cotton, boots and shoes, clothing, hosiery and knit goods, woolens, lumber (sawmills), iron and steel, and slaughtering and meat packing (for the payroll industries).
[b] See note d to Table 4.

Although Table 7 indicates a very large gain in over-all coverage compared with Table 5, in one respect the coverage of the state data is inferior. In almost all cases fewer states are represented. Except for our cotton series, which includes South Carolina beginning in 1910, all of our data are from states east of the Mississippi River and north of the Ohio River and the Mason–Dixon line. Altogether, our interpolating series use data from nine states: Connecticut, Maine, Massachusetts, New Jersey, Ohio, Pennsylvania, Rhode Island,

25

TABLE 7

Coverage of State Data on Average Annual Earnings and Days Worked per Year, Three Industries, Census Years, 1889–1914

	BOOTS AND SHOES[a]				COTTON MANUFACTURES[b]				WOOL MANUFACTURES EXCEPT CARPETS[c]			
	Establishments		Number of Workers	% of Census Employment	Establishments		Number of Workers	% of Census Employment	Establishments		Number of Workers	% of Census Employment
	Number in Sample	% of Census			Number in Sample	% of Census			Number in Sample	% of Census		
1889[d]	474	16.5	40,773	28.7	157	17.3	68,991	31.5	141	9.3	20,888	16.6
1899[d]	803	35.6	78,861	52.1	336	31.8	143,369	47.3	367	28.6	76,565	58.6
1904	766	40.4	87,933	54.9	244	21.1	107,479	34.0	311	29.0	73,213	49.9
1909	1,003	52.3	111,495	56.2	312	23.6	170,391	45.0	463	47.0	97,597	57.8
1914	1,042	53.2	101,490	49.2	450	33.9	172,871	43.9	200	22.7	70,542	43.0

SOURCE: See Appendix A.
a Includes cut stock and findings.
b Includes cotton smallwares and cotton lace.
c Includes felt goods and wool hats.
d Census data exclude custom work and repairing.

26

South Carolina, and Wisconsin. However, the great bulk of the data comes from four of these: Massachusetts, New Jersey, Ohio, and Pennsylvania.

The differences (Table 7) between the percentages of census employment and establishments covered show that our state data come in most cases from establishments that are on the average larger than all census establishments. However, for 1914, the only year in which direct comparison is possible, this size bias is smaller in the state data than in the BLS payroll data. The average number of employees per establishment in the state samples in 1914 was 97 in boots and shoes, 384 in cotton manufactures, and 353 in wool manufactures except carpets. The corresponding census averages are 105, 296, and 186 respectively. A similar comparison for the BLS payroll data was given previously (pp. 21–23).

In moving from daily to hourly earnings, we use daily hours data, obtained by dividing average full-time weekly hours by six. Full-time hours, also called standard or prevailing hours, refer to the normal workweek of the establishment or occupation. They thus differ from actual hours, which often lie below standard hours because of slack work or for other reasons. When actual hours lie above full-time hours the difference is "overtime." We know of no accurate way to measure actual hours before 1914.

For 1909 and 1914, average weekly hours are estimated from frequency distributions of employees given in the censuses of 1914 and 1909. These distributions classify workers by the prevailing number of hours worked per week in the establishments where they are employed. The census data are much superior in coverage to the BLS hours data, but they fail to allow for differences in hours of work within establishments. The differences within industries in full-time hours by occupation as shown by the BLS data are usually small, which suggests that the census data do not err badly in treating establishments as units. The second weakness of the census data is the broadness of some of the class intervals, which, at times, makes it hard to estimate means accurately.

For years other than 1914 and 1909, we use the BLS payroll data on full-time hours, adjusting the series to the levels shown by the census data in these two census years. State data on full-time hours were available for some of our states, but it would have been very difficult to combine them with BLS data in a way that would improve the national estimates derived from BLS data alone.

Because we use BLS full-time hours in our estimates of hourly earnings, our estimates are not entirely independent of Douglas. We feel, however, that it is the estimates of daily earnings that are crucial, and these are independent. Since there is relatively little dispersion in full-time hours in a given industry and state in a given year, estimates of hours derived from different bodies of data are usually extremely close. This is shown by Table 8, which gives estimates of

TABLE 8

Estimates of Average Full-Time Daily Hours by Industry,
from Census Data and BLS Payroll Data, 1909 and 1914

	1909		1914	
	Census[a]	BLS[b]	Census[a]	BLS[b]
Cotton goods	9.90	10.02	9.50	9.47
Woolens and worsteds	9.63	9.65	9.23	9.17
Silk	9.53	9.43	9.18	9.10
Hosiery and knit goods	9.70	9.78	9.18	9.13
Boots and shoes	9.42	9.43	9.13	9.12
Iron and steel	10.64	11.20	10.12	10.92

[a] For methods of estimation see pp. 27 and 36.
[b] Douglas's estimates of full-time weekly hours divided by six. Silk derived from original BLS data using Douglas's method.

daily hours for the same industries derived from census and BLS data for 1909 and 1914. The only appreciable difference is for iron and steel, which probably arises in large part because the BLS data include only certain departments of the industry and are overweighted with continuous-process operations.[10] The table suggests that the sampling problem, which may be important in estimating daily earnings, is relatively unimportant in estimating daily hours.

To the extent that short-time occurs within days, our method fails to take it into account, since we use full-time or prevailing daily hours. To the extent that it takes the form of not working for full days, it is caught in our data on the average number of days in operation per year. Where it occurs within the day, we underestimate hourly earnings because we divide average daily earnings by too high a figure for daily hours. However, checks of our estimates of hourly earnings against various benchmarks, to be presented later, show no

[10] The two estimates for this industry are not entirely independent, since BLS data were used to estimate the mean of the open-end class "over 72 hours" of the census data.

bias in this direction. This suggests that the error is either unimportant or is offset by an unknown error in the opposite direction.

The All-Manufacturing Series

Our estimates of hourly earnings of wage earners in all manufacturing begin with estimates of average annual earnings in census years.[11] To obtain average annual earnings we divide total wage payments by the average number of wage earners. However, before performing this division, we adjusted the data to conform to the present definition of manufacturing. This meant deducting the figures for a number of industries now considered to be outside manufacturing, the most important of which are railroad repair shop products, with 366,000 workers in 1914, and illuminating gas, with 44,000 workers.[12] The purpose of this adjustment is to make the coverage of our estimates comparable with that of National Bureau estimates of productivity in manufacturing. The effect of the adjustment is to reduce average annual earnings by $6 in each census year, except in 1889, when it reduces annual earnings by $4.

For 1889, we also had to adjust the original census figures to eliminate the hand and custom trades. This adjustment makes use of the separate data on factory industries for 1899 given in the *Census of Manufactures* of 1904. It was made for each industry. When the 1899 data showed that an industry was partly a factory industry and partly a hand or custom trade, we applied the 1899 proportions to the 1889 figures. Thus the 1889 employment in awnings was reduced by 24.2 per cent and the total wage payments were reduced by 23.1 per cent, the percentages of employment and wages respectively for the custom trade in 1899, as computed from the 1899 and 1904 Censuses.[13]

11 We consider the census years to be 1889, 1899, 1904, 1909, and 1914. The original census volumes refer to the first three of these as the years 1890, 1900, and 1905, though, by the Census of 1909, the census volumes followed the practice used here in referring to earlier censuses. It is clear that all the 1904 data refer to calendar 1904. The law authorizing the Census of 1900 provided that the information collected should be for the fiscal year ending nearest to and preceding June 1, 1900, but it was stated by the Census Bureau that "a very large proportion of the reports actually made . . . related to the business of the calendar year 1899" (*Census of Manufactures, 1890*, Part I, p. xvii). The practice in 1890 was similar to that in 1900.

12 For a full list of these industries, see Solomon Fabricant, *Employment in Manufacturing, 1899–1939*, New York, NBER, 1942, pp. 213–214. We have not deducted the industry tinplate and terneplate, which appears in this list.

13 Douglas makes the adjustment for hand trades in a single operation. He assumes that for all manufacturing the ratio of earnings of factory workers and hand trade workers combined to those of factory workers alone was the same in 1889 as in 1899 (*Real Wages*, p. 219). This method does not use the information provided by the two

The nature of the census employment concepts have an important effect on our annual earnings figures for census years. The annual earnings figures we would like are total payrolls divided by the number of workers in average daily attendance when the plant was in operation. This is because, at a later step, we divide annual earnings by the number of days in operation to get average daily earnings. The nature of the appropriate average employment concept can be seen more easily by reversing the order of the division: total payrolls divided by days in operation would give average daily payrolls, which, divided by the number of workers in average daily attendance, would give average daily earnings.

The actual census employment figures differ from this ideal in two opposite ways. In 1914 and 1909, employers were asked to report, from time or payroll records, the number of workers employed on the fifteenth day of each month or the nearest representative day. The employment figures for the twelve months were then added, employment in any month in which the plant was not in operation was counted as zero, and the sum was divided by twelve. The first source of error is the inclusion of these zero figures, which results in too low an average employment and too high a daily earnings figure. In effect, time lost during whole months in which an establishment was not in operation is counted twice: once in employment and once in the number of days worked.[14] In seasonal industries such as glass, where

Censuses on the change in relative earnings by industry over the decade. Our correction reduces average earnings in 1889 by about $7 more than Douglas's.

We have further adjusted the 1889 annual earnings series to include logging establishments, which were included in the census of the lumber industry after 1905. The Census of 1905 gives 1899 employment and wages for lumber including logging. We adjusted 1889 employment and wages by the ratios of the 1899 data including logging to those excluding logging.

The adjustments to the 1889 Census data can be summarized as follows: Average annual earnings as computed from the 1889 totals are $445. We reduce this by $4 because of the omission of the "Fabricant industries" (see note 12), by $6 because of the inclusion of logging, and by $18 because of the omission of the hand and custom trades, giving a new average of $417. For the number of wage earners involved in these adjustments, see John W. Kendrick, *Productivity Trends in the United States* (to be published by Princeton University Press for the National Bureau of Economic Research), Table D–8.

[14] An example may make this point clearer. Suppose that, in a given year, an establishment employs 40 men for 25 days a month for 10 months at $1.00 per day, and that it is not in operation during the other two months. The annual payroll of the establishment is $10,000. Its average annual employment will be recorded in the census as 33.3, that is $(40 \times 10) \div 12$. Its average annual earnings per full-time equivalent worker will be $300.00 as computed from census data ($10,000 ÷ 33.3). If average daily earnings are computed by dividing $300.00 by the number of days in operation (250) the result is $1.20, which is an overestimate.

the error on this account is large, we have had to make special corrections to allow for it.

The second source of error is that employers probably included in their count some workers who were on the payroll on the fifteenth day of the month but were not at work or receiving pay on that day. This source of error gives us too high an average employment and too low an average daily wage. Checks, to be reported later, of our hourly earnings figures against data built up from hourly wage rates do not suggest any consistent bias in our estimates and thus lead us to conclude that the sources of error just discussed are, in general, roughly offsetting.

In the years before 1909, the census employment concepts are somewhat different. In 1899 and 1904, employers reported average employment for each month without reference to a particular day. In 1889, the average employment concept was essentially average employment during the time the plant was in operation. Thus the first of the two sources of error is absent in 1889, while the second is not. For this reason, our earnings estimates for the early 1890's may be slightly too low. Checks against other data suggest that the error cannot be large.

For the intercensal years, we used data from the states of Massachusetts, New Jersey, and Pennsylvania as interpolators. The Massachusetts series covers the full period, the Pennsylvania series begins in 1892, and the New Jersey series in 1895. We linked the series at these points to prevent the changes in coverage from affecting the movement of the series.[15] The employment coverage of these series is shown in Table 9.

For 1890–1914 Douglas uses data from five additional states as interpolators of annual earnings: Connecticut, Iowa, Ohio, South Carolina, and Wisconsin. Of these only Ohio has a heavy weight (17 per cent of the total in 1914); the other four combined have 18 per cent of the weight in 1914. We did not use most of these states because they did not publish establishment data on days in operation per year continuously throughout the period.[16]

[15] Several series that, by our definition, are not for manufacturing industries were removed from the state totals in deriving our interpolating series. The most important deductions are as follows: *Massachusetts*, 1890–1907, railroad construction and equipment; 1908–1914, cars built by railroad companies and illuminating gas. *Pennsylvania*, 1908–1914, coal mining; 1913–1914, building trades, plants and flowers, crude oil, natural gas, laundries, mines and quarries, garages, and repair shops (public service). *New Jersey*, 1896–1914, mining (iron ore); 1902–1907, laundries.
[16] The inclusion in our annual earnings series of states that are not included in the series on days in operation might improve the annual earnings series, but could introduce

Our estimates of average annual earnings per full-time equivalent worker in all manufacturing are shown in the first column of Table 10. Chart 1 compares this series with Douglas's corresponding series. The differences are slight. Our estimate is $6 lower in each census

TABLE 9

Coverage of Interpolating Series for All
Manufacturing, Census Years, 1889–1914a

	NUMBER OF WAGE EARNERS (THOUSANDS)			AVERAGE ANNUAL EARNINGS	
	Census Data		State Data	United	Three
	U.S.	Three	Three	States	Statesb
	Total	Statesb	Statesb	Census Data	State Data
1889c	3,631	394d	260d	$417	$425d
1899	4,500	1,277	720	420	430
1904	5,180	1,458	817	471	465
1909	6,261	1,718	1,300	512	514
1914	6,598	1,818	1,745	574	568

SOURCE: See text and Appendix A.
a All data adjusted to exclude industries not now considered part of manufacturing.
b Massachusetts, New Jersey, and Pennsylvania.
c Excludes hand and custom trades and includes logging.
d Massachusetts only.

year, except 1889, because of the difference in the definition of manufacturing, and $17 lower in 1889 as a result of the corrections discussed in note 13 above. One of the few large differences after 1899 occurs in 1910, when our estimate is $20 lower. This difference arises largely because we have corrected an error in the Pennsylvania statistics.[17] Our series also recovers more slowly from the depression of the 1890's and rises more in the boom of 1906–1907.

The second column of Table 10 shows the average number of days

spurious movement into the daily earnings series. Since we want annual earnings only as a means of estimating daily earnings, this would be a net loss. The problem could arise if a state included in the annual earnings series had, say, a rise in annual earnings produced solely by a rise in the number of days in operation so that the true daily earnings were unchanged. If days in operation did not rise correspondingly in the states included in the series on days in operation we would get a spurious rise in daily earnings. Accordingly, at no point in the study do we use annual earnings data for which we do not have corresponding data on days in operation. This decision might have been unwise had it resulted in marked worsening of the annual earnings series. Chart 1 suggests that it did not.

[17] Total wage payments in "oil, crude and refined" are shown as $36,400,990 for only 5,770 workers. This is carried into the all-manufacturing total. Pennsylvania, *Annual Report of the Secretary of Internal Affairs* (1911), Part III, Industrial Statistics, 1910, p. 463. The correct figure, $3,640,990, is shown on p. 400.

per year that establishments were in operation. This is a weighted average of data for the same states used in interpolating annual earnings. Within each state, we computed employment-weighted

TABLE 10

Average Days in Operation per Year, Hours per Day,
and Annual, Daily, and Hourly Earnings,
All Manufacturing, 1890–1914

	Average Annual Earnings[a]	Average Days in Operation per Year	Average Daily Earnings	Average Hours per Day	Average Hourly Earnings (cents)
1889	417				
1890	425	294	$1.44	10.02	14.4
1891	429	297	1.45	10.01	14.4
1892	431	296	1.46	10.04	14.5
1893	410	271	1.51	9.99	15.1
1894	376	272	1.38	9.92	13.9
1895	392	284	1.38	9.97	13.8
1896	393	274	1.43	9.96	14.4
1897	395	284	1.39	9.94	14.0
1898	394	288	1.37	9.97	13.7
1899	420	290	1.45	9.94	14.6
1900	432	289	1.50	9.89	15.1
1901	446	287	1.55	9.84	15.8
1902	474	294	1.61	9.79	16.5
1903	481	291	1.65	9.71	17.0
1904	471	288	1.63	9.68	16.9
1905	487	292	1.67	9.70	17.2
1906	526	297	1.77	9.63	18.4
1907	538	294	1.83	9.60	19.1
1908	482	274	1.76	9.55	18.4
1909	512	289	1.77	9.56	18.6
1910	538	286	1.88	9.49	19.8
1911	545	284	1.92	9.47	20.2
1912	564	290	1.94	9.39	20.7
1913	585	283	2.07	9.36	22.1
1914	574	281	2.04	9.28	22.0

SOURCE: See text and Appendix A.
[a] Per full-time equivalent worker.

averages of days in operation by industries; the all-manufacturing averages published by some of the states are weighted by the number of establishments. (See note 15 for a partial list of industries omitted.) The weights for combining states in census years are census employment in manufacturing. For other years, they are linear interpolations

CHART I

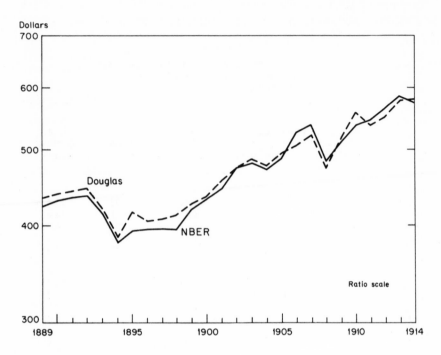

Average Annual Earnings per Full-time Equivalent Worker, All
Manufacturing, 1889–1914

of the census weights. It may help in interpreting these data to mention that the full-time work year during this period was apparently
312 days—365 minus 52 Sundays and one holiday. This can be determined from the data of some states on days in operation by establishments. Establishments operating more than 312 days are listed as
"working overtime," presumably meaning extra shifts.

The Census of 1904 also collected data on days in operation per
year. Table 11 compares estimates based on these data with estimates
based on state data. In each state, the number of days in operation is
lower when estimated from the census data than from the state data
for at least two reasons. First, the census means were computed from
frequency distributions on the assumption that the mean of each class
is the mid-point of the class interval.[18] Since the distribution is
markedly skewed to the left, the errors involved in this assumption are

[18] It was assumed that the mean of the class "30 days and less" was 20 days.

not entirely offsetting and our estimates of the means are under-estimates. More important, the census data are frequency distributions of the number of establishments without regard to size; 9 per cent of these establishments had no wage earners. Where we have examined data on days in operation for establishments classified by number of employees, we have consistently found that large establishments operated more days than small ones. This may be true, in part, because of the greater turnover of small establishments, many of which may have been in existence only part of the year. The inclusion of establishments without wage earners and the overweighting of other small establishments relative to the distribution of employment thus biased the census means downward.

TABLE 11

Estimates from Census and State Data on Days in Operation
per Year in Manufacturing, 1904

	Census Data[a]	State Data
Massachusetts	280	294
New Jersey	283	286
Pennsylvania	272	285
Three-state average[b]	277	288
United States	263	

[a] Computed from *Census of Manufactures, 1905*, Part I, pp. 542–543. For source of state data, see Appendix A.
[b] Weighted by census employment.

The census data suggest that establishments operated more days per year in the three sample states than in the country as a whole. However, this apparent difference could also arise, in part, from the overweighting of small establishments, which are relatively more numerous in the nonindustrial states.

The series on days in operation seems to show a slight downward trend toward the end of the period. The levels reached during the prosperous years 1912 and 1913 are below those of 1890–92, 1902–3, and 1905–7. The series drops during major business contractions, falling below 275 days per year in 1893–94, 1896, and 1908. The drop in 1904 is less pronounced.

Average daily earnings, the third column of Table 10, is obtained by dividing annual earnings by days in operation. Daily earnings rise from 1890 to 1893 and then drop, reaching their lowest point in 1898.

35

The 1893 level is not regained until 1901. Thereafter the rise is steady except for modest declines in 1904, 1908, and 1914.

The behavior of daily earnings for 1892–93 is of a kind found early in cyclical contractions in many of our daily earnings series. Average daily earnings rise, although both annual earnings and days in operation per year fall. This rise in daily earnings could be partly spurious, reflecting some unknown kind of lack of synchronization between the two sets of data from which daily earnings are derived. However, it could also be real, reflecting the concentration of layoffs among low-paid employees and, perhaps, higher output among workers paid at piece rates. Douglas's work shows the same sort of divergence between the movement of annual earnings and hourly earnings in these years. The hourly and daily wage series move downward with a lag of a year in 1894, presumably because of wage cuts.

The fourth column of Table 10 shows average full-time hours per day in all manufacturing. This series will be used again in deriving some of our industry data on hourly earnings. We shall refer to it as the "general hours series." Throughout the study we convert weekly hours to daily hours by dividing them by six. The daily hours figures for 1914 and 1909 were computed from the frequency distributions of full-time hours per week in the *Census of Manufactures*.[19]

From 1903 to 1914 the movement of the general hours series is based on BLS data for seven industries, using Douglas's processing for six of them. The industries are cotton, silk, hosiery and knit goods, woolen and worsted, boots and shoes, lumber, and iron and steel. These were combined by census employment weights, using linear interpolation of these weights for intercensal years. The resulting

---

[19] In computing these means, it was assumed that the mean of the open-end class "48 hours and under" was 48 hours and that the mean of the class "over 72 hours" was 78 hours. The means of all other classes having an interval of more than one hour were assumed to be the mid-points of the class intervals. These assumptions were also followed in all computations of hours per day for individual industries except as otherwise stated.

The assumptions about the open-end classes were made after inspecting BLS bulletins giving more detailed hours data for certain industries. Full-time workweeks below 48 hours in manufacturing were extremely rare before 1914 except in a few rather small industries such as glass, pottery, and newspaper printing. These could not have pulled the mean of the class "48 hours and under" much below 48 hours. Many of the workers in steel and other industries who worked more than 72 hours worked 84, so that the 78-hour mean for this class seems reasonable.

In computing the figures shown, the industries not now considered as manufacturing were deducted from the all-manufacturing totals. In 1914 these deductions made no difference in average weekly hours computed to the nearest tenth of an hour; they lowered the average by 0.1 hour in 1909.

series was then adjusted to pass through the points computed from census data for 1909 and 1914.

This segment of the general hours series uses the hours data for all of Douglas's payroll industries except clothing and slaughtering and meat-packing. For the first of these industries Douglas interpolated the data for 1907–12; for the second, he assumed a constant 60-hour week on the basis of information other than the BLS data. The industry we have added is silk, for which we computed average hours from the BLS bulletins following Douglas's method.[20]

For 1890–1902 the movement of the general hours series is taken from Wolman's series for all manufacturing.[21] This has been linked to the segment of the general hours series for 1903–9 by means of an overlap of one year at 1903. The resulting change in the level of Wolman's series is very small; it has been raised 0.2 hour per week. Wolman's series uses all the hours data for manufacturing in the *Nineteenth Annual Report*; it thus has much broader coverage (48 industries) than Douglas's series, which is derived from the same source for this period, but is confined to 14 industries.

The general hours series as a whole moves downward rather steadily through the period. The average full-time workweek in manufacturing by this measure was 60.1 hours in 1890 and 55.7 hours in 1914. There is a consistent tendency for full-time hours to vary with the cycle, but it is very slight and almost lost in the trend. It may be observed in the small rises in the series in 1895, 1898, 1905, and 1909, all years of recovery from earlier cyclical troughs.

The final column of Table 10 shows our estimates of average hourly earnings in all manufacturing. Chart 2 compares this series with Douglas's series for all manufacturing and for payroll industries. The chart shows a similarity between our series for all manufacturing and Douglas's series for payroll industries that is astonishing in view of the very different sources and methods used, though the payroll series is a bit lower at the end of the period. The Douglas all-manufacturing series, however, lies much above ours as a result of the inclusion of the union industries. This series also falls less and recovers sooner than the other two series in the depression of the 1890's. The over-all rise in percentage terms from 1890 to 1914 is rather similar for the three series. Our series for all manufacturing

---

[20] The more onerous parts of this computation were performed some years ago under the direction of Leo Wolman and were taken from his workbooks.

[21] *Hours of Work in American Industry*, Bulletin 71, New York, NBER, 1938, p. 2.

CHART 2

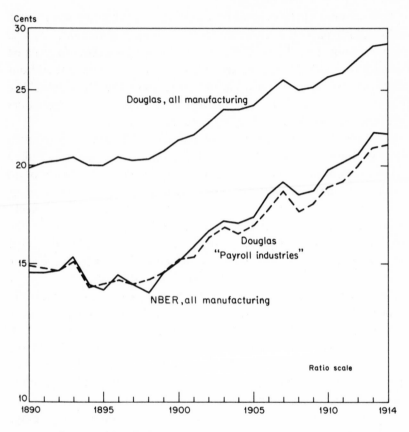

Average Hourly Earnings, All Manufacturing, 1890–1914

rises 52.9 per cent; Douglas's all-manufacturing series rises 44.2 per cent, and Douglas's payroll series rises 43.0 per cent.

At four dates, our figures for average hourly earnings in all manufacturing can be compared with recent estimates by others. Three of the estimates, for 1904, 1909, and 1914, appear in an explanation of the BLS historical series on hourly earnings, though only the last two of these are regarded as part of that series.[22] The BLS estimate for 1904 is 18.2 cents, which is considerably higher than our estimate of 16.9 cents. This BLS estimate is based on occupational wage data for

[22] See "BLS Historical Estimates of Earnings, Wages, and Hours," *Monthly Labor Review*, July 1955, pp. 801–806. This article is based on a memorandum prepared by Witt Bowden.

seventeen manufacturing industries, taken from Bulletin 65 of the Bureau of Labor. Estimated man-hours (census payrolls divided by average hourly earnings) are the weights for combining the industry figures. The industries were selected for completeness of occupational and geographical coverage.

The data of Bulletin 65 are for selected occupations only, and as few as five occupations are represented in some of the industries. Although the selection of industries is such that laborers are included in most cases, the high-wage occupations seem to be overweighted. It would seem preferable where possible to use Douglas's technique for correcting this, which amounts to adjusting the 1904 figures by the ratio of earnings of selected occupations to those of all occupations for 1914.[23]

The BLS estimate for 1909, which is part of its official historical series, is obtained by extrapolating the 1904 estimate to 1909, using as an extrapolator the earnings data from the continuous BLS series for payroll industries. The 1909 estimate is 19.3 cents, compared with ours of 18.6 cents. The BLS estimate for 1914 is obtained by extrapolating the 1909 figures to 1914, using census data on annual earnings and prevailing hours to form an extrapolator. The 1914 estimate is 22.3 cents, compared with our 22.0 cents. What we regard as the upward bias in the level of the 1904 estimate seems to be largely offset by 1914 by some characteristic of the extrapolating series.

For 1890, our estimate of average hourly earnings in all manufacturing can be compared with Clarence Long's, derived from the Dewey Report in the *Twelfth Census, 1900.*[24] Long's estimate is 15.3 cents, compared with ours of 14.4 cents. These estimates are reasonably close considering the great difference in the sources and methods of the two studies. It is difficult to say which is the more accurate. Our estimates are based on state data from only one state before 1892, and our estimate of hourly earnings for 1890 is slightly biased downward by the nature of the census employment count, as explained above. However, the Dewey Report estimates also have several defects, which work in opposite directions. First, the all-manufacturing estimate is a weighted mean of median earnings by

---

[23] See Table 18 for comparisons of our 1904 earnings estimates by industry with Douglas's and with the BLS estimates from Bulletin 65.

[24] Clarence D. Long, *Wages and Earnings in the United States, 1860–1890,* Princeton University Press for NBER, 1960, Table A–8. The data underlying Long's estimate are from Davis R. Dewey, *Employees and Wages,* in *Twelfth Census of the United States, 1900,* Special Reports.

industries. Because the underlying wage distributions are characteristically skewed to the right, their medians will lie below their means. For comparisons with estimates of mean earnings, this biases Long's estimate downward. Second, the industry medians are weighted by the employment shown in the Dewey Report itself, and these overweight high-wage industries. When the industry medians are weighted by employment as reported in the *Census of Manufactures*, the mean for all manufacturing becomes 15.0 cents. Finally, the Dewey Report sampling of firms must be considered. The Dewey Report data are much superior to those of Bulletin 65 in that they cover all occupations in the establishments sampled. However, it is almost uniformly true of such nonrandom samples of wage data that they overweight large or high-wage firms and are, therefore, somewhat biased upward.

If we extend our series backward to 1889 by our methods, we get a figure identical with Long's estimate for 1889. This indicates that the difference for 1890 could result from random fluctuation or error in one of the series—probably ours.

The Industry Estimates

Our estimates of money earnings for individual industries are derived in essentially the same way as the estimates for all manufacturing. However, we have used data from several additional states to estimate the number of days in operation per year and to interpolate annual earnings between census years. These states provided usable data only for some industries or only for short periods of time. Appendix A describes these state data; Appendix B defines the industries and tells which of the state series were used in each of our industry estimates; and Appendix C shows the coverage of the data.

The choice of industries was dictated by the availability of state data. We tried to make estimates for all industries for which there were state data from three or more states covering a substantial part of total employment in the industry. Because we had no data for several leading industrial states, including New York, Michigan, and Illinois, we were forced to omit such important industries as agricultural implements, automobiles, clothing, and meat packing. We did not attempt to include any industry with fewer than 50,000 wage earners in 1914, except that "dyeing and finishing textiles" is included because it is a component of our industry "all textiles." In three industries (electrical machinery, glass, and iron and steel) our interpolators did

40

not go back to 1890; these series begin in 1896, 1899, and 1892, respectively. We attempted to make estimates for some industries (including chemicals, malt liquors, and pottery and clay products) that in the end were omitted because the estimates proved unsatisfactory.

In deriving industry estimates, we met one problem not present in the estimates for all manufacturing. None of the state sources provide definitions or descriptions of the industries to which their industry series refer, and the industry titles at times proved quite misleading. To determine whether or not to use a state series in a particular industry, we compared it at each census year with the census data for the industry in that state. This comparison covered the number of establishments and workers and average annual earnings. Persistent differences in the level of annual earnings combined with incomplete coverage were assumed to reflect sampling bias that would be corrected in large part by adjusting the series to census levels, and thus did not rule out the use of the series. Large differences between state and census data in the movement of annual earnings from one census year to the next were more often grounds for not using a series. It did not prove possible to reduce these criteria for accepting or rejecting state series to mechanical rules.

The New Jersey series "cotton goods" is a good example of a state series that, despite its title, seems to have different coverage than the corresponding census industry. It was not used as an interpolator in cotton manufacturing, though it was used in all textiles. Table 12 shows the "census check" data for this industry.

TABLE 12

Census and State Data for Cotton Goods,
New Jersey, Census Years, 1899–1914

	Number of Establishments		Number of Wage Earners		Average Annual Earnings	
	Census Data	State Data	Census Data	State Data	Census Data	State Data
1899	25	32	5,518	4,728	$342	$282
1904	17	30	5,362	4,917	377	304
1909	26	49	6,638	7,001	388	358
1914	30	41	7,394	7,270	445	405

SOURCE: *Census of Manufactures* and Annual Reports of the New Jersey Bureau of Industrial Statistics.

41

Because it is possible for us to combine series given separately in our sources, but not to break them down, the industry coverage of our series is always that of the broadest of their components. Where census definitions of industries change among censuses, our definition is the broadest of any of the census years. The effect of this is usually to include in an industry various minor auxiliary industries.[25] The inclusion of such auxiliary industries increases the proportion of manufacturing workers covered by our industry estimates. However, it greatly reduces the proportion of census establishments in an industry covered by our series, since the auxiliary industries often include many very small establishments incompletely covered by our state data. The state classification of industries is often finer than that of the census, especially in industries important in the state. The state interpolators are then built up from a number of these state series.[26]

The levels of average daily hours for individual industries for 1909 and 1914 are computed from census data. In two industries, we made special assumptions about the means of the open-end classes in the census distributions. For glass, short workweeks were common for part of the work force, apparently because of the heat and physical strain of some jobs. In this industry we have assumed that the mean of the weekly-hours class "48 hours and under" was 44 hours.[27] For iron and steel the means of the open-end class "over 72 hours" were computed from BLS data.[28]

The movement of hours, except for the trend from 1909 to 1914, is based ultimately on BLS data, combined in several different ways. In five industries (cotton, woolens, hosiery and knit goods, boots and shoes, and iron and steel) we have used the Douglas payroll series adjusted to the census levels of 1909 and 1914. For silk, as mentioned earlier, we computed an hours series using Douglas's methods; this was then adjusted to census levels. The hours series for "all textiles"

[25] Thus we include "glass, cutting, staining, and ornamenting" in the glass industry because it is clear from the number of establishments that it is included in the Ohio series "glass and glassware."

[26] For example, in our industry "leather; tanned, curried, and finished" the Pennsylvania data for 1910–12 show five industries: tanneries, miscellaneous leather, enameled and glazed kid, sole leather, and harness leather.

[27] This assumption is based on inspection of the data for 1907 given in BLS Bulletin No. 77, pp. 40–41.

[28] The means used are 83 hours for blast furnaces and 81 hours for steel works and rolling mills. They are the same to the nearest hour for 1909 and 1914. The estimates are based on the hours data given in BLS Bulletin No. 218, pp. 21–23. The various departments of steel mills were weighted by the employment data for 1915 in *ibid.*, p. 61.

42

is the weighted averages of the series for cotton, woolen, silk, and hosiery and knit goods, with no new adjustment to census levels. In the remaining industries except dyeing and finishing textiles we have used the general hours series described earlier to estimate the movement of hours from 1903 to 1914, adjusting it to the census levels of each industry. For dyeing and finishing textiles we used the "all textiles" series.

In five industries (dyeing and finishing textiles, leather, paper, glass, and foundries and machine shops) for the period before 1903, we used the data for individual industries in the *Nineteenth Annual Report*. For the two remaining industries (rubber and electrical machinery) the data of the *Nineteenth Annual Report* covered four establishments or fewer, and were considered too unreliable to use. We have, therefore, used the general hours series in these industries before 1903 as well as after.

The earnings and hours series for individual industries are presented in Table 13. The rest of this section will discuss features of the individual series.

For seven of our average hourly earnings series it is possible to make comparisons with other estimates covering the full period 1890–1914. Six such comparisons are shown in Table 14 and Chart 3. For four of these (cotton, woolen and worsted, hosiery and knit goods, and boots and shoes) the comparison is with Douglas's payroll series. For silk it is with a series computed from BLS payroll data using Douglas's method. For foundry and machine shops it is with Douglas's union rate series for metal trades; this comparison will be discussed separately after the others.

In three of the comparisons between our series and the series based on BLS payroll data, there are significant differences in level that seem to result from differences in industry definition. In all three, our industry definition is broader and the level of our wage series is lower. In two cases there are also differences between the geographical distribution of the BLS sample and that of the census industry which contribute to the difference in wage levels. The differences in geographical distribution may, in part, result from the differences in industry definition. Another possible source of differences is that our figures are averages for full years, while the BLS data are for one payroll period.

The largest difference in level is for boots and shoes, where in 1914 our series is 3.1 cents an hour below the Douglas series. It can be

43

TABLE 13

Average Daily Earnings, Average Daily Hours, and Average
Hourly Earnings in Fourteen Manufacturing Industries, 1890–1914

	Daily Earnings	Cotton Daily Hours	Hourly Earnings	Daily Earnings	Wool Daily Hours	Hourly Earnings
1890	$1.02	10.31	9.9¢	$1.16	9.98	11.6¢
1891	1.03	10.37	9.9	1.17	9.96	11.8
1892	1.02	10.40	9.8	1.18	9.96	11.9
1893	1.07	10.26	10.4	1.30	9.83	13.3
1894	1.04	10.01	10.4	1.14	9.78	11.7
1895	0.98	10.25	9.5	1.16	9.88	11.8
1896	0.99	10.21	9.7	1.22	9.88	12.3
1897	0.98	10.16	9.7	1.17	9.73	12.0
1898	0.94	10.30	9.1	1.22	9.86	12.3
1899	0.95	10.30	9.2	1.23	9.86	12.4
1900	1.02	10.26	10.0	1.29	9.86	13.0
1901	1.04	10.25	10.1	1.30	9.86	13.2
1902	1.07	10.20	10.4	1.32	9.75	13.5
1903	1.11	10.18	10.9	1.35	9.73	13.9
1904	1.08	10.16	10.7	1.32	9.66	13.7
1905	1.04	10.16	10.3	1.35	9.73	13.9
1906	1.11	10.11	11.0	1.44	9.70	14.9
1907	1.24	10.01	12.4	1.49	9.66	15.4
1908	1.20	9.90	12.1	1.49	9.63	15.5
1909	1.17	9.90	11.8	1.51	9.63	15.6
1910	1.26	9.69	13.0	1.52	9.48	16.1
1911	1.27	9.72	13.0	1.53	9.51	16.1
1912	1.30	9.57	13.6	1.60	9.38	17.1
1913	1.35	9.60	14.1	1.62	9.37	17.3
1914	1.34	9.50	14.1	1.76	9.23	19.0

(continued)

TABLE 13 (continued)

	Daily Earnings	Silk Daily Hours	Hourly Earnings	Hosiery and Knit Goods Daily Earnings	Daily Hours	Hourly Earnings
1890	$1.20	9.95	12.0¢	$0.96	10.13	9.4¢
1891	1.23	10.02	12.2	0.98	10.13	9.6
1892	1.16	9.92	11.7	1.02	10.13	10.1
1893	1.27	9.63	13.2	1.07	10.07	10.6
1894	1.18	9.60	12.3	0.98	9.47	10.3
1895	1.08	9.60	11.2	1.00	10.05	9.9
1896	1.18	9.65	12.3	1.01	10.05	10.0
1897	1.11	9.67	11.5	0.96	10.05	9.5
1898	1.09	9.68	11.3	0.96	10.05	9.6
1899	1.11	9.70	11.4	1.02	10.05	10.2
1900	1.06	9.70	10.9	1.01	9.92	10.2
1901	1.05	9.68	10.8	1.02	9.92	10.2
1902	1.12	9.65	11.6	1.03	9.92	10.4
1903	1.18	9.63	12.3	1.08	9.82	11.0
1904	1.14	9.55	12.0	1.05	9.82	10.7
1905	1.24	9.57	13.0	1.10	9.80	11.2
1906	1.24	9.57	13.0	1.24	9.75	12.7
1907	1.32	9.57	13.8	1.20	9.73	12.3
1908	1.19	9.55	12.4	1.18	9.68	12.2
1909	1.32	9.53	13.8	1.20	9.70	12.4
1910	1.36	9.51	14.3	1.24	9.54	13.0
1911	1.42	9.48	15.0	1.27	9.57	13.3
1912	1.46	9.40	15.5	1.32	9.43	14.0
1913	1.67[a]	9.36	17.9[a]	1.35	9.27	14.6
1914	1.55	9.18	16.9	1.47	9.18	16.0

(continued)

45

TABLE 13 (continued)

	Dyeing and Finishing Textiles			All Textiles		
	Daily Earnings	Daily Hours	Hourly Earnings	Daily Earnings	Daily Hours	Hourly Earnings
1890	$1.54	9.96	15.4¢	$1.08	10.16	10.6¢
1891	1.57	9.96	15.7	1.09	10.19	10.7
1892	1.53	9.89	15.5	1.09	10.20	10.7
1893	1.63	9.74	16.8	1.17	10.06	11.7
1894	1.55	9.57	16.2	1.08	9.83	11.0
1895	1.50	9.75	15.4	1.05	10.06	10.5
1896	1.54	9.75	15.8	1.08	10.05	10.8
1897	1.44	9.60	15.0	1.05	9.99	10.5
1898	1.48	9.77	15.1	1.05	10.09	10.4
1899	1.45	9.77	14.8	1.07	10.10	10.6
1900	1.46	9.77	14.9	1.11	10.06	11.0
1901	1.46	9.77	15.0	1.12	10.05	11.2
1902	1.54	9.77	15.7	1.16	9.99	11.6
1903	1.53	9.77	15.7	1.21	9.95	12.2
1904	1.51	9.79	15.4	1.17	9.92	11.8
1905	1.61	9.82	16.4	1.18	9.93	11.9
1906	1.64	9.76	16.8	1.25	9.89	12.7
1907	1.62	9.73	16.6	1.32	9.83	13.4
1908	1.61	9.65	16.7	1.28	9.75	13.2
1909	1.68	9.66	17.4	1.30	9.76	13.4
1910	1.72	9.52	18.0	1.36	9.60	14.1
1911	1.67	9.56	17.5	1.38	9.63	14.3
1912	1.71	9.43	18.2	1.43	9.49	15.0
1913	1.80	9.43	19.1	1.51	9.48	15.9
1914	1.87	9.31	20.1	1.49	9.35	16.0

(continued)

46

TABLE 13 (continued)

| | Boots and Shoes | | | | Leather | |
	Daily Earnings	Daily Hours	Hourly Earnings	Daily Earnings	Daily Hours	Hourly Earnings
1890	$1.58	9.81	16.1¢	$1.64	9.67	16.9¢
1891	1.57	9.84	15.9	1.70	9.67	17.5
1892	1.58	9.81	16.1	1.67	9.65	17.3
1893	1.60	9.79	16.4	1.65	9.67	17.1
1894	1.57	9.79	16.0	1.54	9.67	15.9
1895	1.51	9.79	15.4	1.56	9.69	16.1
1896	1.47	9.79	15.0	1.57	9.69	16.2
1897	1.44	9.76	14.7	1.56	9.72	16.0
1898	1.39	9.76	14.2	1.51	9.74	15.5
1899	1.42	9.76	14.5	1.47	9.70	15.1
1900	1.43	9.72	14.8	1.48	9.71	15.2
1901	1.47	9.74	15.1	1.49	9.71	15.3
1902	1.48	9.62	15.4	1.50	9.71	15.4
1903	1.57	9.51	16.5	1.53	9.70	15.7
1904	1.55	9.52	16.3	1.56	9.67	16.1
1905	1.64	9.51	17.2	1.54	9.70	15.9
1906	1.66	9.46	17.6	1.67	9.70	17.2
1907	1.75	9.44	18.5	1.73	9.71	17.8
1908	1.74	9.44	18.4	1.72	9.66	17.8
1909	1.73	9.42	18.4	1.76	9.67	18.2
1910	1.83	9.40	19.4	1.81	9.62	18.8
1911	1.86	9.39	19.8	1.87	9.63	19.4
1912	1.89	9.27	20.4	1.81	9.56	18.9
1913	1.93	9.21	21.0	2.14	9.56	22.3
1914	1.94	9.15	21.2	2.04	9.50	21.4

(continued)

47

TABLE 13 (continued)

	Electrical Machinery			Paper and Paper Products		
	Daily Earnings	Daily Hours	Hourly Earnings	Daily Earnings	Daily Hours	Hourly Earnings
1890				$1.30	10.90	12.0¢
1891				1.30	10.87	11.9
1892				1.33	10.87	12.2
1893				1.35	10.83	12.5
1894				1.34	10.89	12.3
1895				1.30	10.89	11.9
1896	$1.57	9.62	16.3¢	1.32	10.87	12.1
1897	1.58	9.60	16.5	1.30	10.94	11.9
1898	1.68	9.63	17.4	1.24	10.99	11.2
1899	1.65	9.60	17.2	1.27	10.38	12.3
1900	1.66	9.55	17.4	1.32	10.38	12.7
1901	1.74	9.50	18.3	1.32	10.20	13.0
1902	1.76	9.45	18.7	1.38	10.13	13.6
1903	1.92	9.38	20.5	1.36	10.22	13.3
1904	1.83	9.35	19.6	1.43	10.17	14.1
1905	1.85	9.37	19.8	1.46	10.27	14.2
1906	1.92	9.30	20.6	1.46	10.23	14.2
1907	1.94	9.27	20.9	1.55	9.81	15.8
1908	1.94	9.22	21.0	1.73	9.76	17.7
1909	1.92	9.23	20.8	1.63	9.78	16.7
1910	2.03	9.18	22.1	1.68	9.71	17.3
1911	2.05	9.18	22.3	1.76	9.70	18.1
1912	2.14	9.10	23.5	1.82	9.61	18.9
1913	2.19	9.09	24.1	1.87	9.59	19.5
1914	2.17	9.03	24.0	1.95	9.51	20.5

(continued)

48

TABLE 13 (continued)

	Daily Earnings	*Rubber* Daily Hours	Hourly Earnings	Daily Earnings	*Glass* Daily Hours	Hourly Earnings
1890	$1.56	9.88	15.8¢			
1891	1.53	9.87	15.5			
1892	1.52	9.90	15.3			
1893	1.61	9.85	16.3			
1894	1.51	9.78	15.4			
1895	1.50	9.83	15.2			
1896	1.57	9.82	16.0			
1897	1.54	9.80	15.7			
1898	1.56	9.83	15.9			
1899	1.55	9.80	15.8	$1.63	9.00	18.1¢
1900	1.53	9.75	15.7	1.76	9.01	19.5
1901	1.58	9.70	16.3	1.82	8.94	20.4
1902	1.54	9.65	16.0	1.87	8.92	21.0
1903	1.54	9.57	16.1	1.81	9.11	19.9
1904	1.56	9.55	16.4	1.96	9.15	21.4
1905	1.59	9.57	16.6	2.08	9.23	22.5
1906	1.72	9.50	18.1	2.04	9.26	22.1
1907	1.70	9.46	18.0	2.10	9.21	22.8
1908	1.84	9.41	19.6	2.15	9.16	23.5
1909	1.84	9.42	19.5	2.05	9.17	22.3
1910	1.95	9.36	20.8	2.17	9.09	23.9
1911	1.96	9.35	21.0	2.22	9.08	24.4
1912	2.01	9.27	21.7	2.25	9.01	25.0
1913	2.06	9.25	22.2	2.35	8.99	26.2
1914	2.20	9.18	23.9	2.34	8.91	26.3

(continued)

TABLE 13 (concluded)

| | Foundry and Machine Shops | | | Iron and Steel | | |
	Daily Earnings	Daily Hours	Hourly Earnings	Daily Earnings	Daily Hours	Hourly Earnings
1890	$1.87	10.10	18.5¢			
1891	1.91	10.10	19.0			
1892	1.87	10.06	18.6	$1.81	10.67	17.0¢
1893	1.88	10.03	18.8	1.84	10.67	17.2
1894	1.86	10.01	18.6	1.70	10.75	15.8
1895	1.81	10.05	18.0	1.64	10.74	15.3
1896	1.78	10.03	17.8	1.68	10.59	15.8
1897	1.73	10.01	17.3	1.64	10.66	15.4
1898	1.76	10.05	17.5	1.69	10.69	15.8
1899	1.73	10.01	17.3	1.90	10.57	17.9
1900	1.79	9.96	18.0	2.01	10.74	18.7
1901	1.79	9.81	18.3	2.10	10.66	19.6
1902	1.88	9.69	19.4	2.16	10.66	20.3
1903	1.93	9.57	20.2	2.16	10.67	20.2
1904	1.91	9.52	20.0	2.03	10.57	19.2
1905	1.93	9.54	20.2	2.07	10.69	19.4
1906	2.02	9.50	21.3	2.17	10.67	20.3
1907	2.07	9.47	21.8	2.30	10.67	21.5
1908	2.06	9.42	21.9	2.25	10.53	21.4
1909	2.08	9.43	22.0	2.34	10.64	22.0
1910	2.15	9.37	23.0	2.46	10.58	23.2
1911	2.20	9.36	23.5	2.57	10.39	24.7
1912	2.24	9.29	24.1	2.56	10.31	24.8
1913	2.33	9.27	25.1	2.82	10.29	27.4
1914	2.33	9.20	25.3	2.70	10.12	26.6

SOURCE: See text and Appendix A.
a Figures for 1913 affected by Paterson silk strike; see note 36.

50

TABLE 14

Comparison of Estimates of Hourly Earnings,
Six Industries, 1890–1914
(cents)

| | Cotton | | Woolen and Worsted | | Basic | Silk Series based |
	NBER[a]	Douglas	NBER[b]	Douglas	Series	on BLS data
1890	9.9	9.7	11.6	12.1	12.0	15.6
1891	9.9	9.5	11.8	12.0	12.2	14.6
1892	9.8	9.5	11.9	12.2	11.7	15.2
1893	10.4	10.1	13.3	12.8	13.2	15.2
1894	10.4	9.5	11.7	11.5	12.3	15.8
1895	9.5	9.4	11.8	11.6	11.2	15.4
1896	9.7	9.9	12.3	11.8	12.3	16.4
1897	9.7	9.6	12.0	12.1	11.5	15.2
1898	9.1	9.3	12.3	12.5	11.3	14.9
1899	9.2	9.2	12.4	12.4	11.4	14.5
1900	10.0	10.3	13.0	13.5	10.9	14.7
1901	10.1	10.4	13.2	13.6	10.8	14.4
1902	10.4	10.7	13.5	13.8	11.6	15.7
1903	10.9	11.1	13.9	14.3	12.3	15.6
1904	10.7	10.9	13.7	13.9	12.0	15.8
1905	10.3	11.1	13.9	14.3	13.0	15.9
1906	11.0	12.0	14.9	15.4	13.0	16.2
1907	12.4	13.5	15.4	16.3	13.8	17.3
1908	12.1	13.4	15.5	15.4	12.4	16.8
1909	11.8	13.0	15.6	15.6	13.8	17.5
1910	13.0	13.3	16.1	15.9	14.3	17.6
1911	13.0	13.5	16.1	16.0	15.0	17.8
1912	13.6	14.8	17.1	17.9	15.5	18.5
1913	14.1	14.9	17.3	17.6	17.9	19.6
1914	14.1	15.3	19.0	18.2	16.9	19.7

(continued)

TABLE 14 (concluded)

	Hosiery and Knit Goods		Boots and Shoes		Foundries and Machine Shops	
	NBER	Douglas	NBERc	Douglas	NBER	Douglas
1890	9.4	11.3	16.1	16.9	18.5	31.9
1891	9.6	11.5	15.9	16.7	19.0	31.3
1892	10.1	10.7	16.1	17.1	18.6	32.3
1893	10.6	10.8	16.4	17.3	18.8	32.2
1894	10.3	10.3	16.0	17.1	18.6	31.2
1895	9.9	11.1	15.4	17.3	18.0	31.3
1896	10.0	10.6	15.0	17.2	17.8	31.7
1897	9.5	10.1	14.7	17.3	17.3	31.7
1898	9.6	10.2	14.2	17.3	17.5	31.6
1899	10.2	10.0	14.5	17.5	17.3	32.2
1900	10.2	10.1	14.8	17.8	18.0	33.2
1901	10.2	10.9	15.1	17.8	18.3	34.0
1902	10.4	11.8	15.4	18.6	19.4	35.2
1903	11.0	12.5	16.5	19.5	20.2	36.3
1904	10.7	12.0	16.3	20.0	20.0	36.4
1905	11.2	12.9	17.2	20.4	20.2	36.6
1906	12.7	13.5	17.6	20.7	21.3	37.8
1907	12.3	14.4	18.5	21.6	21.8	38.9
1908	12.2	14.4	18.4	21.2	21.9	36.7
1909	12.4	14.2	18.4	22.0	22.0	36.9
1910	13.0	14.5	19.4	21.9	23.0	38.6
1911	13.3	14.5	19.8	22.2	23.5	39.6
1912	14.0	15.4	20.4	22.3	24.1	39.9
1913	14.6	16.7	21.0	24.1	25.1	40.6
1914	16.0	17.2	21.2	24.3	25.3	41.3

SOURCE: NBER series from Table 13. Douglas series: Paul Douglas, *Real Wages in the United States, 1890–1926*, Boston, 1930, pp. 96 and 101.
a Includes cotton smallwares and cotton lace.
b Includes felt goods and wool hats.
c Includes boot and shoe cut stock and findings.

CHART 3

Comparisons of Estimates of Average Hourly Earnings in Six Industries,
1890–1914

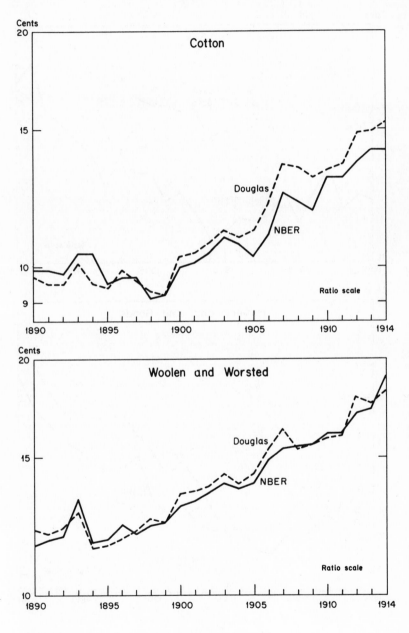

(continued on next page)

CHART 3 (continued)

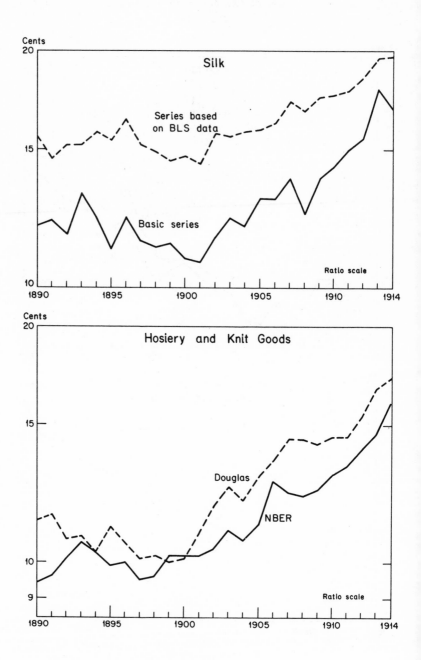

(continued on next page)

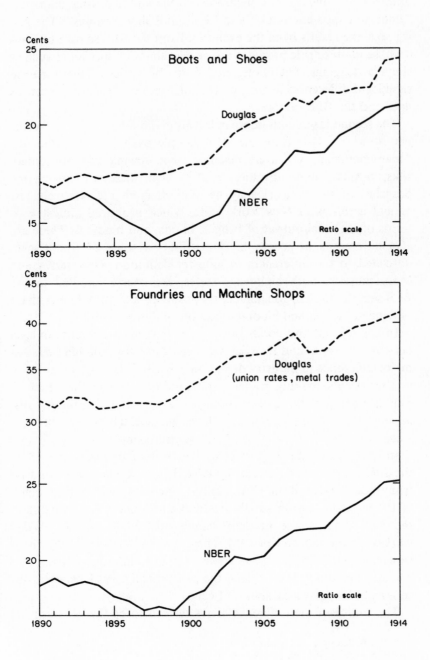

estimated from the 1914 Census data that about 0.3 cent of this difference is due to our inclusion of the lower-paying industries "boot and shoe cut stock" and "boot and shoe findings." The rest we presume results from the exclusion from the BLS sample of firms "whose main or sole products are pegged shoes or specialties such as slippers, leggings, felt boots, etc."[29] In this industry there are no significant differences in geographical distribution between the census data and the BLS sample.

The second largest difference in level is in the silk industry; 2.8 cents per hour in 1914. Here the BLS sample excludes establishments "manufacturing exclusively machine twist, sewing and embroidery silks, braids, laces, novelties, etc."[30] That these are low-paying branches of the industry may be inferred from the relatively low annual earnings in New York State, which produced almost two-thirds of the total output of fringes, braids, and bindings. There are also differences in geographical distribution some of which seem unrelated to the differences in industry definition. New Jersey and Massachusetts, both high-wage states, are overrepresented in the BLS sample, though Massachusetts produced a slightly higher share of fringes, braids, and bindings than of total output.[31]

In hosiery and knit goods there is a rather small difference in level between our series and Douglas's (1.2 cents in 1914), though there is a major difference in industry definition. The BLS data are confined to establishments making hosiery and knit underwear; they exclude establishments making such products as sweaters, bathing suits, gloves and mittens, and jersey cloth. Massachusetts, a high-wage state, is greatly overrepresented in the BLS sample.

In the cotton industry, our series lies below Douglas's after 1899; the difference reaches 1.2 cents by 1914. This difference does not arise from industry definition. Our definition includes two small branches of the industry, cotton smallwares and cotton lace, not included in the BLS data. These branches employed 13,000 of the 393,000 workers in the industry in 1914. They were confined to the northern states and had higher average annual earnings than the industry as a whole. Excluding them widens the difference in 1914 between our series and Douglas's by about 0.1 cent.

The source of the difference seems instead to be the geographical

---

[29] BLS Bulletin No. 232, p. 20.
[30] BLS Bulletin No. 190, p. 195.
[31] *Ibid.*, and *Census of Manufactures, 1914*, Vol. II, pp. 127 and 141–142.

composition of the BLS sample. This sample heavily overweights New Hampshire; it has 19 per cent of the BLS weight and less than 6 per cent of census employment. New Hampshire hourly earnings in the cotton goods industry can be roughly estimated from the census data at 17 cents in 1914, compared with the national average of 14.0. Much of the corresponding underweighting arises from the omission of several states producing relatively small amounts of cotton textiles. The most important of these are Virginia, Maryland, Tennessee, and Mississippi. The average annual earnings of the omitted states as a group are well below the national average, and these states also had a longer workweek than the national average.[32]

In the woolen industry, despite differences in industry definition, there is no appreciable difference in level between Douglas's series and ours. The two do not differ by as much as 1 cent in any year.

The series in each of the five sets just discussed differ in movement as well as in level. The differences in movement are most pronounced in the 1890's. Almost all of our series and many of Douglas's reach a peak in 1893 and then decline rather sharply.[33] However, of the five series based on BLS payroll data shown in Table 14, only two (cotton and woolens and worsteds) follow this general pattern. The Douglas series for hosiery and knit goods is higher both in 1891 and 1895 than in 1893; the silk series based on BLS data is higher in 1895 than in 1893, and Douglas's for boots and shoes shows no appreciable decline during the whole depression of the 1890's. Our series, based on state data for all three of these industries, follows the typical pattern of an 1893 peak and a sharp decline. In boots and shoes the decline is unbroken from 1893 to 1898, in marked contrast to the Douglas series.

These differences in movement seem to be related to the size of the sample in the *Nineteenth Annual Report*. The two payroll series that conform best to the general pattern had the largest samples. The average number of workers covered by these series for 1890–99 was 7,045 in cotton and 3,131 in woolen and worsted. In the poorly

---

[32] See BLS Bulletin No. 239, p. 30 and *Census of Manufactures, 1914*, Vol. II, pp. 21, 26, and 47. The BLS sample is that of identical establishments for which 1914 and 1916 data were secured; it is this sample that governs the level of Douglas's series. New Jersey is included only in cotton finishing; we have not included it among the "omitted states" mentioned in the text.

[33] The declines are typically prolonged as well as sharp. Of our eleven industry series that go back to 1893, the earliest to regain its 1893 level is iron and steel, which does so in 1899. Three industries do not regain their 1893 level until 1906 or 1907 (silk, dyeing and finishing textiles, and leather).

conforming series it was 1,683 in silk, 1,206 in boots and shoes, and 824 in hosiery and knit goods.[34]

During the 1890's, only one of our series for the first five industries shown in Table 14 ever departs appreciably from the general pattern. In cotton, our hourly earnings series remains unchanged from 1893 to 1894, while Douglas's falls. It can be seen in Table 13 that this stability of hourly earnings results from proportional falls in daily hours and daily earnings. The hours series may here be reflecting actual rather than full-time hours, since the fall is reversed in 1895. We may, therefore, have overestimated hourly earnings in 1894 by double counting time not worked, once in the reduction in days in operation and once in the reduction in hours.

Our series for these first five industries reach their low points at different dates; woolens and worsteds in 1894, hosiery and knit goods in 1897, cotton and boots and shoes in 1898, and silk not until 1901. Two of the four series based on BLS data that show clear cyclical declines (boots and shoes does not) have their low points in the same year as our series: woolens and worsteds and silk. The other two, cotton and hosiery and knit goods, reach their lowest point in 1899, somewhat later than our series.

After 1900, there are few differences in movement between the series in the two sets. Our series for boots and shoes declines in the business contraction of 1904 while Douglas's does not, and it does not recover in 1909 from its fall in 1908. Our series for hosiery and knit goods turns down in 1907, two years before Douglas's and one year before most of the series for other industries. This series is dominated by the Pennsylvania data, which show a sharp drop in wages in the hosiery branch of the industry from 1906 to 1907.[35] Our basic series for silk reaches a peak in 1903 and drops during the business contraction of 1904, while the series based on BLS data drops in 1903. In 1913 our basic silk series shows a sharp peak as a result of the Paterson strike.[36] The BLS series rises less from 1912 to 1913 and continues to rise to 1914.

[34] This inference about the effect of sample size is supported by the behavior of the Douglas payroll series not shown in Table 14. Three of these (iron and steel, lumber, and slaughtering and meatpacking) conform to the general pattern. In all three the average sample coverage for 1890–99 is over 2,400 workers. In clothing, the pattern is atypical; wages in 1896 are above those of 1893. Here the sample coverage is 1,043 workers.

[35] Pennsylvania, *Annual Report of the Secretary of Internal Affairs*, Part III, Industrial Statistics, Vol. XXXV, 1907 (1908), pp. 123–124 and 179.

[36] This strike, involving almost 22,000 workers and lasting 22 weeks, was conducted by the Industrial Workers of the World. The Paterson area employed about 25,000 of the

In woolen and worsted, our series fails to fall in 1908, while Douglas's shows the drop characteristic of most of the series. This is one of the instances in which our series for annual earnings and days in operation both fall, but days in operation fall more (see p. 36 above). There is an unusual fall in the Douglas series in 1913 not present in our series. In the cotton industry our series is unusual in that the wage decline of 1904 continues in 1905; the Douglas series shows the typical one-year decline.

We turn now to the final comparison in Table 14, that between our series for foundries and machine shops and the Douglas union-rate series for metal trades. The difference in level is very large throughout the period. In 1890, the union rate series is 72 per cent above ours and in 1914, 63 per cent.

Our definition of foundries and machine shops, though very broad, is considerably narrower than that of the union-rate series for metal trades. In several occupations in the metal trades series, especially blacksmiths and helpers, boiler makers and helpers, and machinists and helpers, most of the rates shown are from railroad repair shops, and there a few quotations from miscellaneous industries such as automobile repairing and breweries.[37] However, this difference in industry definitions seems to account for only a small part of the difference in level between our series and the union-rate series. When we estimate hourly earnings in railroad repair shops for 1909 and 1914 using our usual method of combining census and state data, the estimates lie from zero to 8 per cent above our corresponding

28,000 New Jersey silk workers, including dye-house workers. A detailed account of the strike, highly favorable to the employers, is given in New Jersey, Bureau of Statistics of Labor and Industries, *Thirty Sixth Annual Report* (1914), pp. 175–242. See also S. Perlman and P. Taft, *Labor Movements*, Vol. IV of *History of Labor in the United States*, J. R. Commons, ed. (1935), pp. 274–277.

Our New Jersey series for average earnings in silk, including dyeing, moves as follows for 1912–14 (in cents): 1912, 19.7; 1913, 26.7; 1914, 21.0. This series is overweighted in intercensal years in our national series, since we have data from only three states in our interpolating series after 1904. New Jersey had 26 per cent of the census employment in the industry in 1914, and has 36 per cent of the weight in our interpolating series.

Just why the strike produced this sharp rise in our earnings series is not clear. A wage increase of 5 to 10 per cent was announced at the end of the strike (New Jersey, *Thirty Sixth Annual Report*, p. 227), although the union had been broken. The account in the New Jersey Report also indicates that about 2,000 workers were at work throughout the strike and more were at work during parts of it; these may have been predominantly highly skilled workers, or they may have received extra pay during the strike. Our estimate of earnings would also be raised if, on days when a mill was reported as not in operation, a few workers were present and paid, or if the data included in wage payments amounts paid during the shutdown to the augmented force of company guards.

[37] BLS Bulletin No. 171, pp. 245–267.

estimates for foundries and machine shops. The great bulk of the difference in level must, therefore, be due to other causes. These can be discussed in relation to the union-rate segment of the Douglas series (1907–14) from which the whole series takes its level. First, the union-rate data are confined, generally, to large cities. Second, they cover only eight occupations, six of skilled workers and two of helpers of skilled workers. They omit laborers, apprentices, and many semiskilled occupations.[38] Third, it seems probable that, in a given occupation and city, union rates were above the average wage, either because the union was most successful in organizing high-paid workers or because rates were raised by the unions. As mentioned earlier, Wolman has estimated that only 6.5 per cent of workers in the metal trades (excluding iron and steel) were organized in 1910.[39]

Our series for foundries and machine shops declines more in the depression of the 1890's than the Douglas metal trades series. Our series declines 8.0 per cent from 1893 to 1897, and the metal trade series declines 3.4 per cent from 1892 to 1894. In the business contraction of 1904 our series declines slightly, while Douglas's rises very slightly. However, Douglas's series falls rather sharply in the business contraction of 1908, while ours rises slightly because in Massachusetts and New Jersey days in operation fall more than annual earnings.

The iron and steel industry is the seventh industry in which our series can be compared with others, and here several other series are available. These are shown in Table 15 and Chart 4.

Our estimates lie below Douglas's by about 3 cents an hour in the closing years of the period and about 5 cents an hour early in the period. The movement of the two series is very similar, except that ours fails to fall appreciably from 1907 to 1908. In both level and movement, the series published by the United States Steel and Bethlehem Steel Corporations are much closer to our series than to Douglas's.[40] However, both of these company series rise from 1913 to 1914, which is not true of the other two.

The probable reason for the high level of the Douglas series is that the BLS data do not cover all the departments of the industry. They

[38] State reports from Ohio giving occupational wage data for foundries and machine shops in this period show more than ninety occupations in Cleveland, and additional occupations in other cities.
[39] See p. 20 above.
[40] These two series were derived by dividing total payrolls by man-hours, according to letters received from the two corporations. Bethlehem states that these are actual rather than standard hours, though neither letter explains how man-hours were measured or estimated.

do not cover crucible furnaces, rod mills, or structural shape mills, or the conversion of rolled products into finished products such as wire, pipes and tubes, nails, or bolts. Such conversion was frequently done in the same establishment where the steel was rolled, in which case it

TABLE 15
Average Hourly Earnings in the Iron and
Steel Industry, 1892–1914
(cents)

	NBER	Douglas	U.S. Steel	Bethlehem Steel
1892	17.0	22.2		
1893	17.2	22.9		
1894	15.8	19.9		
1895	15.3	20.7		
1896	15.8	21.2		
1897	15.4	20.3		
1898	15.8	20.5		
1899	17.9	21.8		
1900	18.7	23.4		
1901	19.6	23.8		
1902	20.3	25.4	20.1	
1903	20.2	25.8	20.7	
1904	19.2	24.0	19.2	
1905	19.4	24.5	19.8	20.0
1906	20.3	25.5	20.4	20.0
1907	21.5	26.4	21.4	21.0
1908	21.4	23.9	21.4	21.0
1909	22.0	24.5	21.6	22.5
1910	23.2	26.8	22.4	22.0
1911	24.7	27.3	23.4	23.1
1912	24.8	28.3	23.8	24.8
1913	27.4	30.6	25.2	26.2
1914	26.6	29.8	25.7	27.1

SOURCE: For NBER series, see text. Douglas series: Paul Douglas, *Real Wages in the United States, 1890–1926*, Boston, 1930, p. 101. U.S. Steel: United States Steel Corporation, *47th Annual Report, 1948*, p. 28. Bethlehem Steel: Bethlehem Steel Corporation, *Annual Report, 1954*, p. 19.

is included in the census industry. These departments appear to have lower hourly earnings than the included departments. In addition, the regular BLS data exclude workers not assigned to any department engaged directly in production—the power, mechanical, and yard

61

force. A special BLS study for 1910 shows that such workers were more than one-third of the total and that their average earnings were slightly less than those of "productive" workers.[41]

CHART 4

Average Hourly Earnings, Iron and Steel, 1892–1914

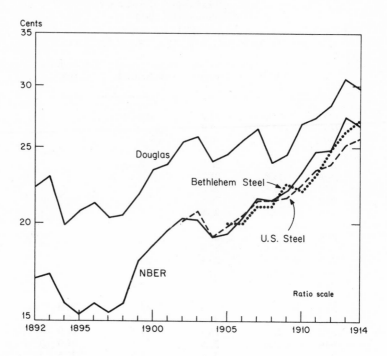

The study just mentioned also permits us to estimate average hourly earnings for the whole industry for May 1910 at 21.6 cents.[42] This is somewhat below any of the figures shown in Table 15 for that year. This figure is also affected by exclusions; the 1910 study omits all plants of the Bethlehem Steel Corporation and also omits departments producing sheet, tin and terne plate, wire, nails, and bolts.

[41] *Report on Conditions of Employment in the Iron and Steel Industry,* Senate Document 110, 62nd Congress, 1st Session (1911), Vol. 1, pp. xxviii–xxix. The average hourly earnings in productive occupations were 22.3 cents; in the power, mechanical, and yard force, 21.0 cents. This last figure was computed from a frequency distribution given in the source.

[42] Computed from the data cited in footnote 41 and a similar frequency distribution for general occupations in the productive departments given in the same table.

Although our earnings estimates for the steel industry are supported by the data available from other sources, our estimates of standard
hours are lower than any others. Table 16 shows three series for
average weekly hours, 1902–14. The comparisons are not extended
back of 1902, since there is only one estimate (Douglas) of the

TABLE 16

Average Weekly Hours in the Iron and
Steel Industry, 1902–14

	NBER[a]	Douglas[b]	U.S. Steel
1902	64.0	67.3	68.4
1903	64.0	67.4	66.6
1904	63.4	66.8	67.4
1905	64.1	67.5	68.9
1906	64.0	67.4	68.6
1907	64.0	67.4	68.5
1908	63.2	66.5	65.1
1909	63.8	67.2	68.8
1910	63.5	67.2	68.4
1911	62.3	66.3	67.2
1912	61.9	66.1	69.0
1913	61.7	66.3	68.9
1914	60.7	65.5	67.6

SOURCE: For NBER series, see text. Douglas series: Paul Douglas, *Real Wages in the United States, 1890–1926*, pp. 96 and 101. U.S. Steel: United States Steel Corporation, *47th Annual Report, 1948*, p. 28.
[a] Standard workweek; Douglas adjusted to census levels in 1909 and 1914; see p. 42.
[b] Standard workweek.

movement of hours available before then. In addition to the estimates
shown in Table 16, an estimate for 1910 of 68.5 hours can be made
from the special BLS study of that year.[43]

If we had used any of these higher estimates of weekly hours and
applied them to our estimates of daily earnings, the resulting hourly
earnings would lie below the other hourly earnings series. There is

[43] *Report on Conditions of Employment in the Iron and Steel Industry*, p. xliii. Average
hours for general occupations and for power, mechanical, and yard force were computed
from frequency distributions. The assumed means of the class intervals were chosen so
as to reproduce as closely as possible the published mean for productive occupations.
Ethel B. Jones has pointed out to us that our hours estimates may be low because they
are benched to census data on prevailing hours of establishments. Within these establishments there were probably departments with longer hours than those of the establishment
as a whole.

some possibility that such an earnings series would be more accurate than the one we have used, since our estimates after 1908 lie above the series on earnings in United States Steel, and these, in turn, were probably above the industry average.[44] On the other hand, the omission of departments making finished products from rolled steel may well explain the higher level of the Douglas hours estimates, while this plus the omission of two other departments with short workweeks, sheet and tinplate, could explain the high level of hours shown by the 1910 study. There are presumably no such omissions in the hours series published by United States Steel. However, in general the workweek for all companies was longest in the departments producing the products where U.S. Steel had the largest share of industry output (ingots and heavy rolled products).[45]

This completes the discussion of earnings series that can be compared with alternative series. For some series already discussed, and some others, comparisons can be made in 1914 with the data published by the National Industrial Conference Board. These comparisons are shown in Table 17, together with Douglas's estimates where available. In two cases, cotton and paper and paper products, the NICB divides our industry into two parts. In both cases, our estimate lies between the two NICB figures, though in both cases a weighted average of their figures lies above ours.[46]

Where direct comparison between our figures and the NICB figures

[44] U.S. Steel had a large proportion of its employment in the Pittsburgh district, which was in general the highest wage district (see *ibid.*, p. xxxiv). Within this district, U.S. Steel employees had higher earnings than those of small companies, but somewhat lower earnings than those of large independent companies. This last statement is based on comparisons of average earnings by type of company in each of five departments (blast furnaces, open hearth furnaces, blooming mills, plate mills, and bar mills) computed from frequency distributions in *ibid.*, Vol. IV, p. 264. Large independent companies ranked first except in open hearth furnaces, where U.S. Steel ranked first. U.S. Steel ranked last in bar mills.

[45] For U.S. Steel's share of output by products in 1913 and 1914 see Temporary National Economic Committee, *Investigation of Concentration of Economic Power*, Part 31 (1941), p. 17,747. The corporation's share of industry production was 50.3 per cent for ingots and 50.6 per cent for rails in 1914, while in sheet it was 39.3 per cent and in tubes and pipe, 44.8. In 1910, the standard workweek of productive workers in tube mills was 62.0 hours compared with 69.8 for all departments (*Report on Conditions of Employment*, p. xliii); in 1914 the standard workweek in sheet mills was 52.3 hours, compared with 64.9 in all departments (Wolman, *Hours of Work in American Industry*, p. 9, computed from BLS data). On the other hand, U.S. Steel produced more than half the industry output of wire rods and tinplate in 1914, and in these departments the standard workweek was also short.

[46] Weighting the NICB cotton figures by census employment in the South and the non-South gives an industry estimate of 15.1 cents. Weighting the NICB figures for paper and for paper products by census employment gives an average of 21.2 cents.

is possible, theirs are higher in six cases and lower in two; in boots and shoes the figures are the same. The largest difference is 3.2 cents an hour in electrical apparatus. In two other industries the difference is between 2 and 3 cents an hour.

There are six industries for which Table 17 permits direct comparisons between three sets of data. In three of these—iron and steel, boots and shoes, and foundries and machine shops—the NICB figure is closer to ours than to Douglas's. The NICB figure for iron

TABLE 17

Comparison of Estimates of Average Hourly
Earnings by Industry, 1914
(cents)

	NICBa	Douglas	NBER
Iron and steel	26.3	29.8	26.6
Electrical apparatus	27.2	n.s.	24.0
Foundries and machine shops	27.8	41.3b	25.3
Cotton, North	17.6⎱	15.3	14.1
Cotton, South	11.7⎰		
Hosiery and knit goods	17.8	17.2	16.0
Silk	19.6	19.7c	16.9
Wool	18.2	18.2	19.0
Leather	21.7	n.s.	21.4
Boots and shoes	21.2	24.3	21.2
Paper and pulp	23.3⎱	n.s.	20.5
Paper products	18.7⎰		
Rubber	25.0	n.s.	23.9

n.s. = not given in source.
a National Industrial Conference Board, *Wages and Hours in American Industry*, New York, 1925, Chapter IV. Data are for July.
b Metal trades, union rates.
c NBER estimate from BLS data, using Douglas's method.

and steel further confirms the level of our estimates for that industry. In the other three industries—hosiery and knit goods, silk, and wool —the NICB data lie closer to the Douglas or BLS figures than to ours. This suggests that in these industries the NICB industry definition is similar to that of the BLS, but this inference cannot be checked directly.

We can also make comparisons for 1904 between some of our industry estimates and BLS estimates from Bulletin 65.[47] Table 18

[47] These are from "BLS Historical Estimates of Earnings and Hours." The methods used in making these estimates are briefly discussed on pp. 38–39.

65

compares these estimates with ours and Douglas's. Our estimates are consistently below those of the BLS, probably because the BLS data are based on wage rates for selected occupations only. The Douglas estimates, though based on the same data as the BLS estimates, are very close to ours for two industries, cotton goods and woolens and worsteds. This is because Douglas, in effect, corrects his 1904 estimates by the 1914 ratio of wages in selected occupations to wages in all occupations. In hosiery and knit goods, the Douglas estimate is somewhat closer to the BLS estimate than to ours, perhaps because

TABLE 18

Comparison of Estimates of Average Hourly Earnings by Industry,
1904
(cents)

	BLS[a]	Douglas	NBER
Cotton goods	13.0	10.9	10.7
Dyeing and finishing textiles	18.0	n.s.	15.4
Foundries and machine shops	24.3	36.4[b]	20.0
Hosiery and knit goods	12.7	12.0	10.7
Leather	17.6	n.s.	16.1
Woolens and worsteds	15.0	13.9	13.7

SOURCE: BLS series: *Monthly Labor Review*, July 1955, p. 802. NBER series: See text. Douglas series: Paul Douglas, *Real Wages in the United States, 1890–1926*, Boston, 1930, pp. 96 and 101.
n.s. = not given in source.
[a] These figures, presented in the source to the hundredth of a cent, have been rounded to the nearest tenth of a cent.
[b] Metal trades, union rates.

the Douglas and BLS data cover a more narrowly defined industry than ours. For foundries and machine shops the Douglas estimate is, of course, much higher than the other two because it has been linked to the series of union rates for the metal trades.

Comparisons of industry estimates for 1890 are also of interest, since this year forms the link between series for earlier periods and those for our period. Table 19 compares our estimates and Douglas's, which extend forward from 1890, with some estimates from the Aldrich Report, which extends backward, and from the Dewey Report. The estimates from the Aldrich and Dewey data are those of Clarence D. Long.

The various sets of estimates shown in Table 19 display no consistent pattern. This is in keeping with the view expressed earlier that the

Dewey Report estimates reflect offsetting biases: the upward bias usually present in small nonrandom wage samples and the downward bias of the median relative to the mean. Both of these biases are present in the estimates from the Aldrich data, the first to a much more marked degree. Our own data, we feel, have a rather uniform slight downward bias. In the eight comparisons of our figures with the Dewey Report medians, ours are lower in three cases and higher

TABLE 19

Comparison of Estimates of Average Hourly Earnings by Industry,
1890
(cents)

	Aldrich Report[a]	Dewey Report[b]	Douglas[c]	NBER[d]
Boots and shoes, factory product	n.s.	17.0	16.9	16.1
Cotton goods	12	10.0	9.7	9.9
Dyeing and finishing textiles	n.s.	12.0	n.s.	15.4
Foundries and machine shops	n.s.	16.0	31.9[e]	18.5
Hosiery and knit goods	n.s.	10.0	11.3	9.4
Leather	16	15.0	n.s.	16.9
Rubber	n.s.	15.0	n.s.	15.8
Woolens and worsteds	13	10.0	12.1	11.6

n.s. = not given in source.

[a] From Clarence D. Long, *Wages and Earnings in the United States, 1860–1890*, Princeton University Press for NBER, 1960. Median of occupational daily wages divided by mean daily hours. Long uses the median for comparability with the Dewey Report data; elsewhere he presents mean daily wages from the Aldrich Report.

[b] *Ibid.*, Table A–8. Median hourly wages.

[c] Paul Douglas, *Real Wages in the United States, 1890–1926*, Boston, 1930, pp. 96 and 101.

[d] See text.

[e] Metal trades, union rates.

in five. The Douglas payroll estimates lie closer to our figures than to the Dewey medians in cotton and wool, and closer to the Dewey medians in boots and shoes and in hosiery and knit goods. The Aldrich Report medians are above the Dewey medians in every case, and above our estimates in two of the three cases. The downward bias of the median seems to be especially important in the Dewey Report data for the woolen industry, where the median earnings are no higher than in cotton or hosiery and knit goods. On all other evidence, wages in the woolen industry lie significantly above wages in these other two industries.

We conclude this section with some comments on a few of the series in Table 13 whose movements have not yet been discussed. It should be noted that "all textiles" is more than the combination of our five series on individual textile industries. It also includes two smaller industries not shown separately: (1) carpets other than rag, and (2) cordage, twine, jute, and linen goods. In addition, the state data used as interpolators include some series that could not be assigned to a particular textile industry, such as "mixed textiles" or "cotton and woolen textiles." For this reason the movement of the series should be somewhat more reliable than that of its components. In computing the all-textile series, we combined data by states and states by census employment.

The series for glass presented unusual difficulties. The number of days worked per year in the glass industry is very low. In 1914, an average of 256 days was worked in the states for which we have data; in other industries the average number of days worked was between 270 and 289. The New Jersey reports mention each year that "closing down for the months of July and August is an established practice in all glass factories," and census data on employment by months in 1914 show that in the glass industry (exclusive of cutting, staining, and ornamenting) employment in the lowest month, August, was only 57.7 per cent of employment in the peak month, March.

Such seasonality in employment would lead us to overestimate daily and hourly earnings if we applied our usual method. The census computes average employment for the year by summing employment for the twelve months and dividing by twelve. If we divide total wage payments by employment so computed to obtain average annual earnings, we have already allowed for the fact that some plants do not operate in the summer months. If we now divide these annual earnings by days worked, we again allow for summer closings, and this double counting of days not worked gives too high a daily wage.[48]

To prevent the overestimation of daily earnings on this account, we have adjusted the census employment figures for glass (exclusive of cutting, staining, and ornamenting, which is part of our series) before computing annual earnings. The adjustment consists of discarding the three months during which employment is lowest

[48] Rather late in our work we discovered that a similar seasonal problem was present in another of our series, pottery and clay products. The brick industry, a major component of this series, is highly seasonal, and we could devise no satisfactory method of allowing for this. Accordingly, the series for pottery and clay products was discarded.

68

(July, August, and September) and using the average employment for the remaining nine months.

Because this adjustment is somewhat arbitrary, we needed an independent check on the level of our series for glass. Such a check is afforded by the Dewey Report.[49] The Dewey Report data for glass for 1899 (the year ending June 1, 1900) cover 6,148 workers, out of a total industry employment of 52,818. The data cover the middle-Atlantic, central, and southern states and do not exclude any occupations. We have combined the three frequency distributions of wage rates per hour (for males 16 and over, females, and males under 16) for all areas and occupations and computed the mean of the combined distribution, which is 18.9 cents. This lies between the figures for 1899 (18.1 cents) and 1900 (19.5 cents) of our basic series, and suggests that the adjustment described in the preceding paragraph is an appropriate one.

The cyclical movement of our series for glass is unusual and may not be reliable. The trough in 1903 is a year earlier than for most industries, while the trough in 1909 is a year late (see Table 13). Exactly the same movements in 1903 and 1909 appear in the series for paper and paper products. For both industries, in key states in 1908, there are declines in employment and days in operation without corresponding declines in annual earnings.

The period 1890–1914 is one in which a number of new industries were growing rapidly. Unfortunately, we were unable to get state data for most such industries and they are not well represented in our industry series. For the industries shown in Table 13, there is no clear relation between the rise in wages and the rate of growth in employment. However, by looking within the rubber industry, we can contrast the wage movement of the old, stable branches with that of a new, rapidly growing branch. The old branches are rubber boots and shoes and rubber hose and belting; the new branch is rubber, not elsewhere specified (n.e.s.), which by 1910 consisted largely of rubber tires and tubes. Although we do not have separate series on these branches for 1900–1910, we can approximate them closely by state

[49] *Employees and Wages*, pp. 482–483. The Dewey Report is greatly superior to the *Nineteenth Annual Report* in that for most industries it has considerably larger samples of workers, and its data cover all the workers in the establishments sampled. It has not been widely used because it covers only two years (the years ending June 1, 1890 and June 1, 1900) and because the basic data are presented as detailed frequency distributions for which medians are the only averages given. The distribution of hourly wage rates for glass has seventy-four classes, most of them one cent wide.

series. In 1909, Ohio had 39 per cent of employment in rubber, n.e.s., and was unimportant in the other two branches. The production of rubber boots and shoes was highly concentrated in Massachusetts, and that of rubber belting and hose in New Jersey. Table 20 shows the movement of daily earnings and of census employment in the rubber industry in these three states for 1899–1910. The earnings series are the state data before adjustment to census levels. Such adjustment would lower the level of the Ohio series somewhat,

TABLE 20

Average Daily Earnings and Wage Earner Employment in the
Rubber Industry, Three States, 1899–1910

| | Average Daily Earnings | | | Number of Wage Earners | | |
	New Jersey	Massachusetts	Ohio	New Jersey	Massachusetts	Ohio
1899	$1.54	$1.58	—a	3,385	11,510	3,505
1900	1.58	1.55	$1.45			
1901	1.58	1.70	1.51			
1902	1.60	1.57	1.72			
1903	1.62	1.57	1.81			
1904	1.68	1.61	1.80	3,920	12,677	4,815
1905	1.63	1.66	1.82			
1906	1.64	1.76	2.04			
1907	1.77	1.70	1.92			
1908	1.90	1.86	2.04			
1909	1.80	1.81	2.08	6,550	10,346	11,065
1910	1.81	1.85	2.31			

SOURCE: See Appendix A.
a Not shown; sample inadequate.

but would not affect its movement appreciably. The faster rise in earnings in Ohio is undoubtedly related to the faster growth of employment; a large part of it comes early in the period, suggesting that the beginning stages of the rapid expansion caused the greatest labor shortages.

Beginning in 1899 we have series for thirteen industries excluding "all textiles." From 1899 to 1914 there is a very slight tendency for the earnings differentials among these industries to narrow. The coefficient of variation of the thirteen average hourly earnings figures drops from 21 per cent in 1899 to 19 per cent in 1914.

The Combined-Industry Series

In this section we combine the industry average hourly earnings series of the preceding section into a weighted average which serves as a check on the all-manufacturing series. We cannot make a similar check for average daily hours because the hours series for all manufacturing and for the individual industries are based on the same data. However, for earnings, the all-manufacturing series covers a much wider range of industries than the individual industry series do, while the latter include data from a number of states not used in the all-manufacturing series.

In combining the industries series we treat "all textiles" as one industry; it already includes the separate series for the other textile industries. "All textiles" and the eight nontextile industries of the preceding section are combined using census employment weights with linear interpolations of weights between census years. The industry series that do not go back to 1890 are brought in by linking so as not to disturb the movement of the combined series. The resulting series for nine industries combined is compared with the all-manufacturing series in Table 21 and Chart 5.

The two series never differ by more than one cent. The all-manufacturing series lies 0.1 cent below the nine-industry series in 1890 but rises until it is 1.0 cent higher in 1913, indicating that industries whose wages rose less than the average are overrepresented in the nine-industry series. The principal difference in movement occurs in the business contraction of 1908, when the nine-industry series rises slightly while the all-manufacturing series falls. The rise in the nine-industry series throughout 1907–09 occurs despite the fact that all but two of its components (leather and foundries and machine shops) fall either from 1907 to 1908 or from 1908 to 1909. However, only three fall between the first pair of years, and three others rise sharply. The sharp rises are in paper, rubber, and glass; in each case, in the leading states, employment and days in operation fall, but days in operation fall more than annual earnings.

The nine-industry series was also computed with constant 1914 weights. We have not shown this series here, since it never differs by more than 0.1 cent from the variable-weight series. This indicates that the rather considerable differences among the industries in rates of growth of employment are not strongly related to wage levels. This lack of relation was confirmed by examining a scatter diagram in

71

which percentage changes in employment from 1899 to 1914 were plotted against 1914 average hourly earnings, with the principal component industries of all textiles plotted separately.

TABLE 21

Average Hourly Earnings in All Manufacturing and in Nine
Manufacturing Industries Combined, 1890–1914
(cents)

	All Manufacturing	Nine Industries
1890	14.4	14.5
1891	14.4	14.7
1892	14.5	14.6
1893	15.1	15.2
1894	13.9	14.5
1895	13.8	14.0
1896	14.4	14.2
1897	14.0	13.9
1898	13.7	13.9
1899	14.6	14.3
1900	15.1	14.8
1901	15.8	15.2
1902	16.5	15.8
1903	17.0	16.3
1904	16.9	16.1
1905	17.2	16.3
1906	18.4	17.1
1907	19.1	17.8
1908	18.4	17.9
1909	18.6	18.0
1910	19.8	18.9
1911	20.2	19.4
1912	20.7	20.0
1913	22.1	21.1
1914	22.0	21.2

SOURCE: All Manufacturing: Table 10. Nine Industries: computed from Table 13.

72

CHART 5
Average Hourly Earnings, All Manufacturing and Nine Industries
Combined, 1890–1914

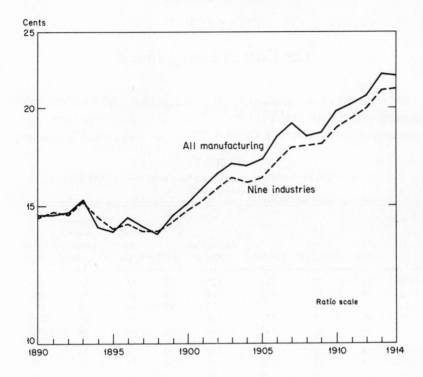

CHAPTER 4

The Cost-of-Living Index

THE new cost-of-living index for the period 1890–1914 and its component indexes are presented in Table 22. The more important components are also plotted in Chart 6. The index is designed to measure

TABLE 22

The NBER Cost-of-Living Index and Its Components, 1890–1914

(1914 = 100)

	All Items	Food (Douglas)	Clothing	Home Fur-nishings	Rent	Fuel and Light	Liquor and Tobacco (Douglas)	All Other Items
1890	91	72	134	122	93	83	81	106
1891	91	72	135	119	93	86	83	107
1892	91	70	135	117	95	84	80	107
1893	90	72	128	114	95	84	81	105
1894	86	69	118	110	93	76	84	100
1895	84	68	113	103	90	78	87	97
1896	84	66	113	100	91	83	86	98
1897	83	68	110	96	88	80	85	95
1898	83	69	107	96	88	78	89	93
1899	83	70	106	95	87	79	92	93
1900	84	71	108	95	85	91	93	95
1901	85	74	103	93	87	92	96	94
1902	86	78	99	91	86	100	96	93
1903	88	77	98	93	91	112	95	96
1904	89	78	97	90	96	105	96	97
1905	88	78	96	87	97	101	98	97
1906	90	81	98	89	98	101	98	98
1907	94	85	102	96	102	101	98	101
1908	92	83	97	94	99	101	100	98
1909	91	84	95	95	97	100	100	97
1910	95	91	97	95	99	99	98	98
1911	95	93	96	96	97	95	99	97
1912	97	96	99	97	97	99	100	98
1913	99	97	101	98	100	102	98	100
1914	100	100	100	100	100	100	100	100

SOURCE: See text except for Douglas's indexes, which are from his *Real Wages in the United States, 1890–1926*, Boston, 1930, pp. 36 (food) and 609 (liquor and tobacco).

74

changes in the prices paid by manufacturing wage earners for consumer goods, though it may also prove useful for some broader purposes. We begin the discussion with Douglas's food index and our unsuccessful attempts to improve on it. We then discuss in some detail our new indexes of the retail prices of clothing and home furnishings based on mail-order catalogues. These indexes fall

CHART 6

Principal Components of the NBER Cost-of-Living Index, 1890–1914

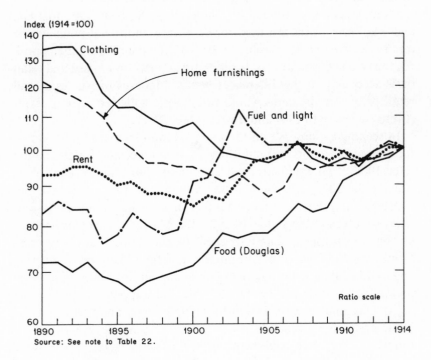

Source: See note to Table 22.

between 1890 and 1914, although the wholesale prices of clothing and home furnishings rise—a pattern we do not entirely understand. Next we deal with our new index of rents based on newspaper advertisements, and our index of the prices of fuel and lighting, a composite of old and new data. We return to Douglas to pick up his index of prices of liquor and tobacco and then discuss the weighting of the components.

Our cost-of-living index rises considerably less than Douglas's, and this is the main source of the rise in real wages found in this study. At the close of the chapter, we consider whether the index is biased in one direction or the other and cannot find a basis for thinking that either bias is more probable.

Food

Douglas's "most probable index of the relative cost of food to working-men" is based on the retail prices of twenty-nine foods from 1890 to 1907[1] and of fifteen of these foods from 1907 to 1914. The fourteen omitted items are continued by wholesale prices from 1907 to 1914, and wholesale prices are used for seventeen additional items whose retail prices were not collected by BLS at any time during the period. All thirty-one of the wholesale series are adjusted to a presumed retail basis according to the differences between indexes of wholesale and retail prices for the items whose prices were collected at both levels (twenty-seven until 1907 and thirteen thereafter).

In seeking to improve on the Douglas food index, we looked first for sources of additional retail price series, especially for the period after 1907. Two such sources were found. For June of each year, starting in 1898, the New Jersey Bureau of Industrial Statistics collected the prices of a large number of food items in seventy-four cities or towns in the state.[2] In 1920, the Massachusetts Commission on the Necessaries of Life published the retail prices of thirty-seven food items for each month beginning in 1900.[3] The quotations were apparently taken from records of retailers; no information is given on the locations within the state to which they apply.

To determine whether to substitute New Jersey and Massachusetts retail prices for wholesale prices wherever possible, we made the following test. For each item whose national retail prices were available after 1907 we plotted annually, beginning in 1898, the retail series for the two states, the national retail series, and the wholesale series. We then judged from the charts whether the state retail data or the BLS wholesale data more closely approximated the national

---

[1] The retail prices of thirty items were collected by the Bureau of Labor during this period. However, Douglas did not use the series for veal, apparently because his budget weights did not permit him to separate expenditures on veal from expenditures on mutton and lamb. Elsewhere he deals with problems arising from the absence of weights by using simple averages of all the available series.

[2] The prices of forty-two items were collected throughout 1898–1914 if different grades of the same commodities are counted separately. Seven items had been added by 1914.

[3] *Report*, 1920, pp. 123–141 and 154–172.

retail series. Somewhat surprisingly, the state retail data for both states were, on the whole, not better approximations of the national retail data than were the wholesale data. Although the state retail data were markedly better approximations for a few items, they were markedly worse for an equal number. All of the other series tended to fluctuate more than the national retail and, in some cases, the state retail fluctuated more than the wholesale series. This tendency in the New Jersey retail series probably arises because they are for a single month in each year, whereas the wholesale are averages of monthly data. The erratic movement of some Massachusetts series may be due to the use of quotations from a very small number of stores. Other Massachusetts series, however, are suspiciously stable.

Our final decision was not to use any state data on food prices. We turned next to the weighting of the food index. Douglas's weighting pattern for food expenditures is taken from the *Eighteenth Annual Report of the Commissioner of Labor* (*Cost of Living and Retail Prices of Food, 1903*) and is summarized in the second column of Table 23. It seemed unusual because of the very small proportion of the food budget spent on starchy foods. One explanation for this is the relatively high income of the families whose budgets were studied. The average annual income of the 2,567 families that reported food expenditures in detail was $827, while that of all 25,440 families covered in the study was $750. For the larger group the average income from the earnings of the husband alone was $621. In contrast, our estimate of average annual earnings in manufacturing in 1901 (the year covered by this budget study) is $446.[4]

The *Sixth* and *Seventh Annual Reports of the Commissioner of Labor*[5] provide a source of data on food expenditures in which family income can be roughly controlled by selecting sets of data, since the data are given separately by the industry in which the

[4] The rough standard that the income from the earnings of the husband should be about equal to the average annual earnings in manufacturing involves two opposite sources of error: (1) Our annual earnings estimates are "full-time equivalent" earnings based on the average number of workers employed for the whole year, and not on the total number of individuals employed at any time during the year. However, some husbands in budget-study families must have been ill or unemployed during part of the year, and their earnings would, therefore, be lower than full-time equivalent earnings; (2) The average earnings of all manufacturing workers include the earnings of women, children, and single men, which tend to be lower than those of husbands. Because the second of these errors probably predominates, we prefer to select a set of families from the budget study such that the income of husbands is slightly above the manufacturing average.

[5] *Cost of Production: Iron, Steel, Coal, Etc.*, 1891, and *Cost of Production: The Textiles and Glass*, 1892.

77

principal breadwinner worked. If we exclude the data for two high-wage industries, we are left with a sample in which the average income from the earnings of husbands is close to that of all manufacturing workers. The seven industries included are cotton, woolens, pig iron, steel, iron ore, bituminous coal, and coke; the excluded high-wage industries are glass and bar iron. The average earnings of

TABLE 23

Summary of Food Expenditure Patterns from Budget Studies,
1890–91 and 1901
(per cent)

| | Per Cent of Total Food Expenditure | |
	1890–91[a]	1901[b]
Meat	27.8	28.4
Poultry and fish	1.4	5.4
Eggs	3.3	5.1
Dairy products	14.6	16.1
Lard	2.7	2.9
Coffee and tea	5.9	4.9
Sugar and molasses	8.1	5.3
Flour and meal	13.5	5.1
Bread	2.1	3.8
Rice and potatoes	3.8	4.6
Vegetables	3.7	5.8
Fruit	1.8	5.0
Vinegar, pickles, and condiments	0.3	1.3
All other	10.9	6.2
Total	99.9	99.9

[a] Computed from *Cost of Production: Iron, Steel, Coal, Etc., Sixth Annual Report of the Commissioner of Labor* (1891), and *Cost of Production: The Textiles and Glass, Seventh Annual Report of the Commissioner of Labor* (1892). Data apply to families with heads-of-household working in the seven industries listed in the text.

[b] Computed from *Cost of Living and Retail Prices of Food, 1903, Eighteenth Annual Report of the Commissioner of Labor* (1904).

husbands in the seven industries (weighted by the number of families in the sample) was $450. Our estimate of the average annual earnings in all manufacturing industries in the years apparently covered by these budget studies is $430 for 1890 and $434 for 1891.

The first column of Table 23 summarizes the food expenditures pattern for 1890–91 of families in these seven industries. This pattern gives a substantially heavier weight to starches and sugar than the pattern for 1901. From 1898 to 1914 there were divergent movements

78

in the prices of various foods. The prices of meat, poultry, and eggs and dairy products rose sharply, while the prices of flour and bread rose much less, and the price of sugar fell. It seemed possible, therefore, that a change in weighting patterns would materially alter the movement of the index. This, however, did not prove to be true. When we measured price changes over the whole period of rising prices from 1898 to 1914 using the two sets of weights summarized in Table 23 we got almost identical results. This happened because the 1890–91 pattern gives lower weight than the 1901 pattern to rice, vegetables, fruits, vinegar, and fish, all of which had smaller than average price rises. The lower weights of these items offset the effect of the heavier weights for starches and sugar.

The 1890–91 weighting pattern thus seems better in principle than the 1901 pattern because it applies to families whose income is more like that of all manufacturing workers. In practice, however, the choice of weights makes so little difference that we did not bother to recompute the entire index. In the end we accepted the Douglas food index without change. It is shown, converted to the base 1914 = 100, as the second column of Table 22.

Clothing and Home Furnishings

The methods used in constructing the clothing and home furnishings components of our cost-of-living index are very similar, and they will, therefore, be discussed together.

For both clothing and furniture Douglas used BLS wholesale group indexes as his basic indexes. To dampen their fluctuations, these were adjusted by the differences between wholesale and retail price indexes for identical food items. The use of the wholesale group index "cloths and clothing" to represent retail clothing prices involves some special difficulties.[6] First, this group index includes some items (carpets, sheetings, and blankets) that would not be classified as clothing in the consumer budget studies. This leads to the underweighting of the true clothing items and the overweighting of home furnishings. More important, "cloths and clothing" includes several items or groups of items that would almost never be bought by consumers without further processing (leather, four series; linen

---

[6] The wholesale group indexes for 1890–1914 were revised by BLS from time to time. The versions used by Douglas in *Real Wages*, Appendix B, can be reproduced by converting the indexes given in *Wholesale Prices, 1890–1919*, BLS Bulletin 269, July 1920, to the base 1890–99 = 100.

shoe thread; raw silk, two series; scoured wool, two series; worsted yarn, two series; and cotton yarn, two series). The price behavior of these raw materials and semifinished goods may be quite different from that of finished clothing or of yard goods.

Our indexes of the retail prices of clothing and home furnishings are constructed from data from the catalogues of Sears, Roebuck and Company and Montgomery Ward & Company. The use of mail-order data for retail price indexes is, of course, not new. W. I. King used Sears data in constructing a cost-of-living index for 1909–28 which was published in the bulletins of the National Bureau of Economic Research. More recently, mail-order data were used in the Meany-Thomas report during World War II in an attempt to show that the BLS cost-of-living index was biased.[7] The adverse appraisals of the Meany-Thomas report have tended to cast doubt on the use of mail-order data. However, the defect in the Meany-Thomas mail-order indexes was not the source of data, but the way in which items were selected. These were, on the whole, much lower priced than those typically bought by moderate-income urban families and quality was often not held constant. When the BLS selected items at prices deemed representative of those paid by the urban families covered in its budget studies of 1935–36, it obtained indexes of mail-order prices very similar to the corresponding components of the cost-of-living index.[8] We have attempted to profit from this experience by selecting items priced at levels shown by the 1918 budget study[9] to be typical for urban families in a relevant income range.

Apart from the question of price levels, it may be asked whether any other bias arises from the use of mail-order prices, since mail-order buying was more typical of rural than of urban areas during our period. We cannot detect any such bias. The catalogue prices are f.o.b. Chicago and do not include freight to rural areas. The catalogues cover a full range of items suitable for urban working- or middle-class families. The names or descriptions of many items are designed to appeal to such nonfarm workers as engineers, carpenters, plumbers,

[7] George Meany and R. J. Thomas, *Cost of Living*, Washington, January 1944. Meany and Thomas were the labor members of the President's Committee on the Cost of Living.

[8] See President's Committee on the Cost of Living, *Report*, 1945, pp. 51–54, 325–327, and 356–357. The conclusion that the mail-order prices selected by the BLS verified the general BLS indexes was that of a technical committee whose members were Wesley C. Mitchell, chairman, Simon Kuznets, and Margaret G. Reid.

[9] *Cost of Living in the United States*, BLS Bulletin 357. None of the budget studies before 1918 give itemized data on purchases of clothing or home furnishings.

miners, and teamsters. The available evidence suggests that the gross margins of mail-order houses were similar to those of urban department stores.[10] Moreover, catalogue prices are prices at which transactions actually take place—they are not lowered by discounts or bargaining.

In selecting the items for our indexes we began with the general list of items used by the BLS in its cost-of-living index after 1914. These items were selected by BLS from the 1918 budget study. The list contained seventy-one clothing items and twenty-two home furnishings items.[11] We followed the BLS in pricing clothing for a family of four: husband, wife, a twelve-year old boy, and a girl of six. Eventually, we reduced these lists to thirty-six clothing items and nineteen furniture items by dropping items whose prices we could not follow, whose weights proved to be very low, or which could be well represented by a closely similar item. The list used is given in Appendix D.

We have two price series for fourteen of our nineteen furniture items and for about half of the clothing items. The purpose of trying to get two price series for each item was to allow for attrition in following prices back through the catalogues and to provide a wider range of styles and qualities. Only one series was attempted, however, if the item had little weight in the index and if the 1918 budget study showed little variation in the average expenditure per article at different income levels.

In constructing each price series we first selected from the 1918 Sears catalogue the specific variety of the item to be priced.[12] Where possible, the specific varieties were chosen so that the price of one was about equal to the average expenditure per article for all families covered in the 1918 budget study and the price of the other, to the average expenditure per item for families in the income class whose average expenditure was lowest.[13]

[10] See Table 30.

[11] The full list is given in National Industrial Conference Board, *The Cost of Living*, New York, 1925, pp. 75–77.

[12] For example, for men's cotton union suits, basic item 1 under clothing, there were more than forty styles or qualities in the catalogue, ranging in price from 54 cents to $1.98. We chose a long-sleeved combed cotton union suit at $1.48 (specific item 1a) and a long-sleeved Swiss-ribbed lisle at $1.42 (specific item 1b).

[13] This is usually, but not always, the lowest income class. The asymmetrical choice of income classes was made because of the high level of average incomes of the families covered by the 1918 budget study. The average income from earnings of the husband of all families in the study was $1,349. One of us has estimated elsewhere that the average annual earnings per full-time equivalent worker in manufacturing in 1918 were $1,077

It is a serious disadvantage of our procedure that we select items on the basis of a budget study that not only lies outside the period we cover, but is separated from it by the violent price rises caused by World War I. The average expenditure per article for many items was undoubtedly affected by wartime changes in relative prices. However, we had no alternative to the 1918 study.

We attempted to select specific items that were durable and serviceable rather than fashionable. Thus, we usually selected warm, heavy clothing and simple furniture. This, incidentally, made it easier to follow prices, since such items were less affected than others by changes in style.

Once our specific items had been selected for 1918, we followed them back through the catalogues from year to year. We used only one each year for a given item, usually the fall general catalogue. For a few items that seemed likely to be bought in the spring, such as refrigerators or summer underwear, we used the spring general catalogue. Since the great majority of our items were priced in the fall catalogue, which is released during the summer, the indexes can be said to represent prices at about the middle of each year.

In general, it was possible, from the combination of descriptions, pictures, and catalogue numbers, to follow items of given quality with reasonable certainty. As we got into the earlier part of the period, the descriptions became less adequate and our task more difficult. Several items had to be dropped because they could no longer be followed.

Whenever the specific variety of an item disappeared from the catalogue, we substituted a similar one, at as nearly the same price as possible, using an overlap of one year. When the price series was computed, we linked the two segments to remove the change, if any, in price level. Only two of our series have no such links; the largest number for any is eight. The number for each series is shown in

(A. Rees, *New Measures of Wage-Earner Compensation in Manufacturing, 1914–57*, New York, 1960, NBER, Table 9). The income bias appears to be built into the selection of families. Agents were instructed to exclude, among others, families with boarders and "slum or charity families or non-English speaking families who have been less than five years in the United States" (Bulletin 357, p. 2). We are indebted to Margaret G. Reid for calling this point to our attention. See also note 4.

For men's cotton underwear, which can again serve as an example, the average expenditure per article by husbands was $1.58 for all income classes and $1.41 for the income class "under $900." The range of expenditures by income class is, of course, much narrower than the range by families. It can, nevertheless, be wide for some items. For chairs and stools the average expenditure per item in all families was $3.90; for families in the income class "under $900" it was $1.92.

82

Appendix D. Occasionally, these links involved a major change in the character of the item. For example, no gas stoves appear in Sears catalogues before 1902, and we used a coal cooking stove before that time. Appendix D notes all such major changes.

In all cases we began following items in 1918 in the Sears catalogues only.[14] When we could no longer follow any appropriate style or quality of the item, we switched to Ward catalogues and tried to follow the item there. Items that first appeared in Sears catalogues after 1900 could usually not be found in Ward catalogues any earlier. Before 1900, however, the Ward catalogues were much more complete. The 1890's was a period of rapid growth and change for Sears;[15] Ward, in contrast, was a well-established and stable firm. The Ward catalogue contained a full range of clothing and home furnishings throughout the 1890's. Sears carried only watches and jewelry before 1894. Thus, for 1890–93 our indexes use Ward data only, for 1894–1900 they are mixed, with the proportion of Sears data increasing; after 1900 they are based predominantly on Sears data.

When we had two or three specific series for a basic item, we computed simple averages of these series before weighting them. (In Appendix D these are designated by letters such as 1a and 1b; the number refers to the basic item.) If one specific series ended before the other, the remaining one was linked to the average.

For many of the clothing items in the BLS list we were unable to use our usual procedure because frequent shifts in fabric and style prevented following any one style for more than a year or two. For the five most important of these items we used an alternative chain-index procedure.[16] These items were men's wool suits, women's wool suits, women's wool coats, women's housedresses or wrappers, and women's cotton waists.[17] For these items we selected five specific styles in 1918 that could be followed back to 1917, and computed the simple average of the percentage changes. For 1917 and 1916 we repeated the procedure using, for the most part, different specific

[14] We began with Sears catalogues because they were available in the University of Chicago Library and the New York Public Library and because by the end of our period, Sears was much the larger of the two houses.

[15] See Boris Emmet and John E. Jeuck, *Catalogues and Counters*, 1950.

[16] We are indebted to Mrs. Ethel D. Hoover of the Price Division of the Bureau of Labor Statistics for suggesting this procedure to us.

[17] We substituted cotton waists for the silk waists in the BLS list because Bulletin No. 357 shows that silk waists were more important than cotton only for families with incomes above $1,200 a year.

83

items, and so back for each pair of years.[18] The percentage changes were then linked, forming a chain index. In a few cases the number of items included in a link was fewer than five if five could not be followed. It was not possible in the chain indexes to relate price levels to the average expenditures in 1918. For men's suits, women's cotton waists, and women's housedresses, the items in the chain indexes remain fairly stable throughout the period. For women's wool coats, the styles changed rather rapidly. Before 1904, capes and jackets were more common than full-length coats.

Before 1906 ready-to-wear women's suits did not appear consistently in the catalogues of either house. We therefore used a composite index of wool serge yard goods and trimmings (buttons, braid, and satin lining). These components were followed by our usual method rather than the chain-index method. The yard goods were given a weight of 8, the lining, 2, and braid and buttons, 1 each.[19]

Because chain indexes are sometimes subject to cumulative error or "drift" we have computed an alternative clothing index in which the chain items are omitted. In this version the composite index for women's suits described in the preceding paragraph is used throughout 1890–1918. The weights of the other chain items are reassigned to other series, in large part to yard goods. The two versions of the index are compared in Table 24. The index excluding chain items lies below the other before 1913 and above it in 1917–18. The largest difference (9 points) occurs in 1891–92. The basic trends of the two versions are quite similar. We decided to use the version including the chain items, since it incorporates additional information that seems to have some value.

For both the clothing and home furnishings indexes we used weights based on the expenditures of families with incomes under $1,500 in 1918, as reported in the 1918 budget study. The average expenditures per family for the three income classes "under $900," " $900 and under $1,200," and " $1,200 and under $1,500" were combined in a

---

[18] As an example of the procedure, we may describe the series for housedresses for 1916–18. For the link from 1918 to 1917, the five items were a standard percale, a checked flannelette, a cotton serge stout, a striped gingham, and a checked gingham. The first, third, and fifth could also be followed from 1917 to 1916. The other two were replaced by a figured flannelette and a chambray stout.

[19] These weights are based on the relative share of cloth and trimmings, respectively, in the total cost of a ready-to-wear woman's suit whose wholesale price was below $20. The costs were reported to the Tariff Board by seventeen large New York City manufacturers. See *Wool and Manufactures of Wool*, Report of the Tariff Board on Schedule K of the Tariff Law, House Document 342, 62nd Congress, 2nd Session, 1912, pp. 892–898.

TABLE 24

Alternative Versions of the Clothing Price Index, 1890–1918
(1914 = 100)

	Including Chain Items	Excluding Chain Items
1890	134	126
1891	135	126
1892	135	126
1893	128	120
1894	118	112
1895	113	108
1896	113	108
1897	110	104
1898	107	102
1899	106	101
1900	108	104
1901	103	100
1902	99	95
1903	98	94
1904	97	94
1905	96	93
1906	98	95
1907	102	99
1908	97	94
1909	95	94
1910	97	95
1911	96	95
1912	99	98
1913	101	101
1914	100	100
1915	101	100
1916	111	111
1917	146	148
1918	186	191

SOURCE: See text and Appendix D.

simple average.[20] For home furnishings, the items included in our index account for about 58 per cent of all expenditures on home furnishings for these income groups. The remaining expenditures are largely on items very unlike the included items. The most important

[20] An average weighted by the number of families in each class would have over-weighted the highest class. For general discussion of the income bias in this budget study, see note 13.

excluded groups are dishes and glassware, kitchen utensils, brooms and brushes, lamps, pianos, "talking machines," and toys.[21] We did not attempt to assign the weights of omitted articles to specific included articles; thus, the included items carry the weights of omitted items in proportion to their own importance. The weights for the home furnishings index are shown in Table 25.

TABLE 25

Weights for the Home Furnishings Price Index

	Average Expenditure per Family, 1918	Per Cent of Total Weight
Carpets	$3.07	11.3
Linoleum	1.22	4.5
Chairs	1.94	7.1
Tables	1.34	4.9
Couches	1.36	5.0
Dressers and chiffoniers	1.03	3.8
Buffets and china closets	0.84	3.1
Bedsteads	1.70	6.3
Bed springs	0.74	2.7
Mattresses	1.45	5.3
Blankets	1.29	4.7
Sheets	1.11	4.1
Pillowcases	0.54	2.0
Stoves	4.54	16.7
Refrigerators	0.67	2.5
Tablecloths	0.27	1.0
Towels	0.48	1.8
Baby carriages	2.13	7.8
Sewing machines	1.47	5.4
Total	$27.19	100.0

SOURCE: *Cost of Living in the United States*, BLS Bulletin 357, pp. 392–401. The dollar amounts are simple averages of expenditures per family for the three lowest income classes.

For the clothing index it seemed desirable to account explicitly for omitted items, since the included items represented a much smaller part of total expenditures. We therefore divided all clothing items into the twelve categories which define the rows of Table 26, and each of these was further divided into men's, women's, and children's items. In each of the resulting thirty-six cells we entered the expenditure on

[21] These items are also omitted from the BLS index after 1914. Except for pianos and talking machines, Bulletin 357 does not give average expenditure per article, which may explain their omission by BLS.

TABLE 26

Distribution of Basic Clothing Items and
Expenditures by Categories

Category	Men's Expenditures[a]	No. of Items[b]	Women's Expenditures[c]	No. of Items[b]	Children's Expenditures[d]	No. of Items[b]
Hats and caps	$2.61	2	$3.42	0	$2.80	0
Woven wool outerwear	14.83	2	9.18	2	11.91	4
Woven cotton and silk outerwear	9.71	3	11.47	3	13.44	2
Knit cotton clothing, except hosiery	3.03	1	2.64	2	4.57	2
Knit wool clothing, except hosiery	1.92	1	0.50	0	2.34	1
Hosiery	3.00	1	2.25	1	5.65	1
Corsets, garters, and suspenders	0.60	0	1.57	1	0.56	0
Nightwear, handkerchiefs, and woven underwear	0.92	1	2.55	0	2.27	0
Shoes and other leather products	12.66	1	8.66	1	20.52	2
Rubbers and other rubber goods	1.17	1	0.29	0	1.35	0
Celluloid collars and cuffs	0.55	1	none	0	0.12	0
All other items	1.85	0	1.73	0	1.03	0
Total	$52.85	14	$44.26	10	$66.56	12

[a] From *Cost of Living in the United States*, BLS Bulletin 357. Average expenditures of husbands per family, simple average of averages for the three lowest income classes.
[b] Number of basic items in our price index in 1918. Some items are represented by two price series.
[c] Average expenditures of wives per family, computed as for husbands.
[d] Sum of average expenditures per family for male children, 12 years and under 15 years, and female children, 4 years and under 8 years, computed as for husbands.

such items by our hypothetical family of four (husband, wife, boy of twelve, and girl of six). These were the simple averages of average expenditure per family for the three lowest income classes of the 1918 budget study. Table 26 shows for each cell, first, these average expenditures and, second, the number of basic items priced that fall in the cell (not the number of separate price series or specific items, which is larger).

We assigned weights to items in three steps. First, the expenditure

87

in the empty cells (those in which we priced no items) were assigned to the full cells on the same row.[22] If there was one empty cell and two full cells in a row, the expenditures in the empty cell were divided equally among the full cells. Second, the average expenditures in each cell, including those added in the first step, were assigned to the items in the cell in proportion to expenditures on them. Third, we totaled the expenditures in each column after step two. Because the first column (men's) had the fewest empty cells, it was relatively over-weighted. It has been found in more recent price studies that the prices of children's clothing sometimes move differently from those of other clothing. We therefore adjusted all the weights in each column to restore the column totals. The weights in the first column were multiplied by approximately 0.81, those in the second column by approximately 1.15, and those in the third column by approxi-mately 1.12.[23] The weights for each item resulting from this procedure are shown in Table 27. When, in moving back through time from 1918,

TABLE 27

Weights for the Clothing Price Index
(per cent)

	Per Cent of Total Weight
Man's	
Union suit, cotton	1.54
Cap, winter	0.97
Hat, felt	3.51
Coat	1.51
Suit, wool[a]	6.03
Overalls or work pants	1.46
Shirt, cotton	2.80
Union suit, part wool	1.11
Nightshirt	2.92
Socks, cotton	1.53
Shoes	6.44
Rubbers	1.43
Collar, celluloid	0.34
Necktie	0.68
Total	32.27

(continued)

[22] For example, we did not price women's hats or children's hats and caps. In step one, the expenditures on these items are assigned to men's hats and caps.

[23] We are indebted to Dorothy S. Brady for suggesting this three-step weighting procedure.

88

TABLE 27 (concluded)

	Per Cent of Total Weight
Woman's	
Coat, wool[a]	3.68
Suit, wool[a]	2.93
Housedress or wrapper	4.49
Waist, cotton[a]	1.46
Corset	1.96
Corset cover	0.62
Union suit, cotton	1.28
Stockings, cotton	1.62
Shoes, high	6.24
Total	24.28
Child's	
Boy's mackinaw or reefer	1.77
Boy's pants, cotton	1.91
Boy's pants, wool	1.75
Union suit, cotton, 12-year	2.64
Union suit, wool, 12-year	1.82
Stockings, cotton, 12-year	3.96
Boy's shoes, high	12.92
Girl's coat, winter	3.45
Girl's shoes, low	1.47
Underwaist, 6-year	0.57
Total	32.26
Yard Goods	
Wool serge[b]	1.21
Gingham[c]	8.51
Voile[d]	1.46
Total	11.18
Total, all groups	99.99

SOURCE: Computed from Table 26.
a Item priced by chain-link method.
b Given weight of girl's wool dress.
c Given weight of girl's cotton dress, woman's apron, and girl's apron.
d Given half of weight of woman's cotton waist.

an item disappeared from the index we reassigned its weight to a similar item and eliminated the change in level by linking.

The years 1915–18, although they lie outside the period of this study, had to be included in the clothing and home furnishings indexes to enable us to use the 1918 budget study in selecting our items. This also permits comparison of our indexes for 1914–18 with those of the BLS and the NICB. The comparisons are shown in Table 28; they indicate generally close agreement on the size and timing of price rises during World War I.[24]

TABLE 28

Comparisons of Retail Price Indexes for Clothing and
Home Furnishings, 1914–1918
(1914 = 100)

| | | Clothing | | Home Furnishings | |
	NBER	BLS[a]	NICB[b]	NBER	BLS[a]
1914	100	100	100	100	100
1915	101	102	103	100	105
1916	111	112	120	113	117
1917	146	134	143	132	136
1918	186	176	177	176	179

SOURCE: National Industrial Conference Board, *The Cost of Living*, New York, 1925, pp. 34 and 111; NBER indexes, see text and Appendix D; BLS indexes, see text note 24.
a Adjusted to midyear; see text note 24.
b July of each year except 1918; 1918 figures are for June.

Before 1914 we can compare our indexes only with components of the wholesale price index. These comparisons are shown in Table 29 in the columns headed "all items." Our indexes are surprisingly different from the wholesale indexes. While both wholesale indexes are lower in 1890 than in 1914, both of ours are substantially higher. All fall from 1890 to 1897, and all rise from 1905 to 1914. However, in the intervening years, 1897–1905, the trends diverge: the retail indexes continue to fall, while the wholesale rise.

24 The BLS indexes for 1914–17 were based on price data for eighteen shipbuilding centers and for Washington, D.C. for December of each year. For December 1917–December 1918, data were collected for thirteen additional cities. The change from the average prices of 1913 to those of December 1914 was estimated from wholesale price movements and the indexes for December of each year were published on the base 1913 average = 100. The estimated change from the 1913 average to December 1914 was only 1 per cent for clothing and 4 per cent for home furnishings. To get the figures shown in Table 28 we have averaged the BLS data for Decembers of adjacent years, obtaining series that refer roughly to the middle of each year, as ours do. The 1914 base figures for these series were obtained by averaging the December 1914 figures and the estimated 1913 figures.

The NICB (*The Cost of Living*), did not publish a separate index for home furnishings, which it included in sundries. It first collected clothing prices in 1918; the prices for earlier years were apparently collected in 1918 from retailers' records.

TABLE 29

Comparison of Retail and Wholesale Price Indexes for Home Furnishings and Clothing, 1890–1914
(1913 = 100)

| | HOME FURNISHINGS | | | | CLOTHING | | | |
| | All Items | | Common Items | | All Items | | Common Items | |
	NBER Retail	BLS Whole-sale	NBER Retail	BLS Whole-sale	NBER Retail	BLS Whole-sale	NBER Retail	BLS Whole-sale
1890	124	72	92	72	133	94	123	93
1891	122	72	90	73	134	91	129	94
1892	120	71	90	70	133	91	128	92
1893	116	68	87	70	126	88	124	90
1894	112	67	79	64	117	78	107	78
1895	105	62	74	60	112	78	107	76
1896	102	58	75	58	112	75	104	76
1897	98	56	78	58	109	75	104	73
1898	97	61	78	61	106	79	99	72
1899	97	62	80	63	105	82	98	76
1900	97	69	86	72	107	88	97	82
1901	95	69	85	69	102	82	96	78
1902	92	73	86	70	98	84	90	80
1903	95	74	86	73	97	88	89	84
1904	92	73	88	75	96	89	92	84
1905	89	71	86	77	96	91	88	85
1906	91	74	92	80	98	97	96	92
1907	98	80	100	86	101	104	102	97
1908	96	78	96	83	96	94	92	89
1909	97	77	97	81	94	98	90	94
1910	97	80	98	85	96	99	93	100
1911	98	85	100	87	96	96	93	98
1912	99	91	98	93	98	98	96	97
1913	100	100	100	100	100	100	100	100
1914	102	99	99	98	99	98	100	99

SOURCE: For the list of items common to the full wholesale and retail indexes, and for the sources of the retail all-items index, see text and Appendix E; wholesale all-items indexes for house furnishing goods and for cloths and clothing from *Wholesale Prices, 1890–1919*, BLS Bulletin 269.

Some of the difference between the movement of the two clothing indexes, and much of that for the two furniture indexes, can be explained by the differences in the selection of items. The wholesale home furnishings index consists of thirteen items, of which only three (chairs, tables, and bedroom sets) have counterparts in our index. The remaining nine consist of glassware, earthenware, table cutlery,

91

and woodenware (pails and tubs). On the other hand, our index includes many items that do not appear in the wholesale index. Some, such as sewing machines, refrigerators, stoves, bedsprings, mattresses, and linoleum, are wholly unlike any items in the wholesale index.

Table 29 includes indexes of the prices of items common to the wholesale and retail price indexes. The two indexes of common items for home furnishings consist of six items each; both are weighted by the weights of our retail index. The items are carpets, wooden chairs, tables, bedroom sets,[25] blankets, and sheets.[26] The wholesale series for carpets, blankets, and sheets are part of the wholesale group cloths and clothing.

The wholesale index for these six items common to the two main indexes is very similar to the wholesale group index for house furnishing goods. However, the retail index for common items is unlike the full retail index and much more like the wholesale index. Like the wholesale index it is higher in 1914 than in 1890, and it begins to rise in the mid-1890's.

The difference between the two retail indexes seems reasonable. The full index, which includes more highly fabricated articles, reflects more of the growth of productivity in manufacturing and less of the rise in price of such materials as lumber and wool. Three of the four metal items in the full retail index (stoves, sewing machines, and metal bedsteads) continued to fall in price from 1897 to 1905 and contributed substantially to the continued fall of the index in these years, whereas the wholesale index and the indexes of common items contained no metal items before 1907. On the other hand, when the wholesale prices of hardwood lumber rose sharply from 1897 to 1905 so did the prices of all wooden items in the wholesale home furnishings index and in the retail index of common items and of most of the wooden items in the retail index for all items.

The wholesale index for cloths and clothing contains several series for raw materials and semifinished goods and some series that we classify as home furnishings. It gives much more weight to yard goods than our index does, and includes no children's clothing. The finished clothing included is limited to underwear, hosiery, and shoes. Thus,

[25] The wholesale series for bedroom sets includes a bedstead, dresser, and washstand. The bedstead is wood until 1907 and iron thereafter. Our series is an index of the sum of the retail prices of a dresser and a bedstead; we did not price washstands. We switch from a wood to a metal bedstead in 1907 to maintain comparability.

[26] For a more complete description of the items common to the full wholesale and retail indexes, see Appendix E.

our retail series for such items as suits, dresses, coats, shirts, overalls, collars, and hats have no counterpart in the wholesale index.

The two indexes of common items for clothing shown in Table 29 consist of seven items each, weighted as in our retail index. The items are all-wool dress goods, gingham yard goods, men's shoes, women's shoes, men's cotton hose, women's cotton hose, and men's wool union suits.[27] Again there is very little difference between the wholesale index of common items and the full wholesale index. The retail index of common items lies somewhat closer to the wholesale index than does the full retail index, but the general pattern continues to resemble the latter and the lowest point is, again, not reached until 1905. The retail index of common items for clothing includes none of the items for which we used the chain-index method, and this may explain much of its divergence from the all-items index (compare Tables 24 and 29).

For both clothing and furniture, the differences in the selection of items do not explain the full divergence between the retail and wholesale indexes. In clothing, the difference between the two indexes of common items remains large.[28] It should be mentioned, however, that the correspondence of items in these comparisons is very rough, and the wholesale index covers a much wider range of qualities. Thus, in men's shoes for 1918 the two retail prices per pair were $4.45 and $4.95, while the three wholesale prices were $1.51, $5.44 and $5.63. There may also be more changes in quality in the wholesale series. Thus, in the comparison for all-wool dress goods our series is wool serge throughout; the wholesale series is Franklin sackings for 1890–1907, Panama cloth for 1907–13, and storm serge for 1913–18 (for other items, see Appendix E).

In seeking to explain the divergent movements of wholesale and retail prices of similar items, we first considered the possibility that retail gross margins of mail-order houses fell during the period. However, the available direct evidence suggests that just the opposite was true. We can get data on margins for a mail-order house only for 1902–5. These are compared in Table 30 with the margins of two large department stores for the same years. The Sears margins are quite similar to Macy's and slightly below those of Marshall Field and Company. If the Sears margins fell substantially relative to those of

[27] For a full description, see Appendix E.
[28] There are, also, large differences between the wholesale and retail price series for most of the items in these indexes considered individually.

TABLE 30

Gross Margins of Three Large Retailers, 1902–1905
(per cent)

	Sears, Roebuck and Company[a]	R. H. Macy and Company[b]	Marshall Field and Company[c]
1902	25.7	23.2	26.6
1903	23.9	24.6	28.0
1904	25.0	25.2	28.9
1905	24.0	26.1	28.1

[a] Boris Emmet and John E. Jeuck, *Catalogues and Counters*, Chicago, 1950, p. 175.
[b] R. M. Hower, *History of Macy's of New York*, Cambridge, Mass., 1943, p. 390.
[c] Computed from R. W. Twyman, *History of Marshall Field and Company*, Philadelphia, 1954, pp. 161, 175–176.

department stores before 1902, they must have been higher to begin with, and this does not seem likely.

The available evidence on the trend of gross margins in other relevant branches of retail distribution is summarized in Table 31. All of it points to rising gross margins during our period. Annual data on Macy's margins for 1890–1914 and Field's for 1890–1906

TABLE 31

Gross Margins of Retailers of Clothing and Home
Furnishings, 1889–1919
(per cent)

	1889	1899	1906	1909	1919
Department stores	22.2	25.6	n.a.	29.3	32.8
Furniture stores, independent	30.6	31.2	n.a.	31.2	39.0
Dry goods stores	19.2	21.4	n.a.	27.0	29.0
Apparel stores	25.4	27.5	n.a.	29.6	31.8
R. H. Macy and Co.	19.5	22.4	26.9	28.4	32.7
Marshall Field and Co.	26.5[a]	27.7	28.7	n.a.	n.a.

Source: Lines 1–4 from Harold Barger, *Distribution's Place in the American Economy*, Princeton University Press for NBER, 1955, pp. 160 ff.; line 5 from Hower, *History of Macy's*, pp. 256, 390; line 6 computed from Twyman, *History of Marshall Field and Company*, pp. 161, 175–176. The Macy data are included in Barger's series for department stores, but the Field data are not.
n.a. = not available.
[a] 1890.

show the same trend.[29] Thus, the movement of gross margins not merely fails to explain the difference between the wholesale and retail price indexes; it widens the difference to be explained.

A second explanation of the differences between the movement of the wholesale and retail indexes relates to the way in which they were constructed. The specific items in the wholesale index were selected at the beginning of the period and followed forward in time until they were no longer important in the market. The items for the retail index were selected at the end of the period and followed backward in time until they disappeared from the market. The retail index will thus tend to include new items sooner after their introduction, at a time when their price may be falling relative to the prices of all items because of the improvement in production processes or economies of scale. The wholesale index will tend to retain for a longer time items that are disappearing from use and whose prices may be rising relative to the prices of all items as the scale of production contracts.[30] We could have tested the effect of this difference by constructing a second retail index on the opposite principle, but this would have involved the collection of much additional price data.

Finally, we must consider the extent to which the divergence between the wholesale and retail indexes results from error in the indexes. In the wholesale indexes, the commodities are specified more precisely than in the retail index and, therefore, may be more comparable through time. Failure to recognize changes in quality in constructing the retail index leads to a price constancy bias—the tendency is to follow a similar commodity at the same price when the price of the identical commodity may have changed. Since the index is constructed backward through time, this may lead us to understate price rises by an upgrading of quality as we move backward during that part of our period in which prices were rising.

Both the retail and wholesale indexes have frequent links in the individual price series made on the basis of a one-year overlap. These also introduce possibilities of error if a link is made in a year when

29 See the sources cited in the notes to Table 31.
30 An example of this difference in timing can be given from among our "common items." During the period covered by our indexes, union suits gradually replaced shirts and drawers for men and boys, as judged by their share in the number of underwear items listed in the mail-order catalogues. Our index includes men's wool union suits beginning in 1898; the wholesale index does not introduce them until 1912. In 1903, the retail price of union suits dropped substantially, while the wholesale price of shirts and drawers was unchanged. Since the items involved are very similar, we cannot be too confident that the general explanation given in the text applies to this case.

one of the segments linked has a rise or fall that might have been recognized from continuous data as part of a temporary peak or trough not present in the other segment. Since such errors tend to be random, the larger the number of series in the index, the greater the likelihood that they will be offsetting. On this ground, our home furnishings index may be somewhat more reliable than the wholesale index. The retail home furnishings index is based on thirty-three series, of which twenty cover the entire period. The wholesale index is based on only thirteen series. For the clothing series, such a comparison is difficult. The total number of series is somewhat larger in the wholesale index, but relatively few are for finished clothing.

Rent

The Douglas cost-of-living index does not include a rent component. We know of two previous rent indexes covering the period, one of which we discovered before we constructed our own, and the other only afterward. The first is given in Carl Snyder, *Business Cycles and Business Measurements*,[31] and covers 1875–1913. It is described as a "special study on rents by the Russell Sage Foundation, unpublished" but nothing whatever is said about the nature of the underlying data or the methods of construction. We were unable to learn more about it by direct inquiries to the Russell Sage Foundation, though we got the impression that the Foundation's statisticians now regard it as unreliable. The index often does not change for many years; for example, it remains at 84 (1913 = 100) from 1880 to 1894. It rises 7.5 per cent between 1879 and 1895, a period of falling prices.[32]

The second rent index for this period is that of *The Real Estate Analyst*.[33] This index is based on advertised rents for single-family dwellings in several cities. No information is given on the number of cities or the number of dwellings covered, or on the methods of constructing the index. The index is charted but not given in numbers.

[31] 1927, pp. 137, 291.

[32] Despite the peculiar movement of this index and the absence of any information about its sources, it has been used in at least two recent studies—Leo Grebler, D. M. Blank, and Louis Winnick, *Capital Formation in Residential Real Estate*, Princeton University Press for NBER, 1956, p. 407 and E. H. Phelps Brown and S. V. Hopkins, "The Course of Wage-Rates in Five Countries, 1860–1939," *Oxford Economic Papers*, n.s. II, 1950, pp. 270–271.

[33] A monthly magazine published in St. Louis by Real Estate Analysts, Inc. The rent index for 1890–1914 is shown in the issue of January 1938, pp. 850–851. It is used in Robert F. Martin, *National Income in the United States, 1799–1938*, New York, NICB, 1939, pp. 99 and 131.

Our own index, which is also based on advertised rents, was already completed when we discovered this one, and we were struck by the strong similarity in movement. Our index rises from 1890 to 1893, and then falls sharply until 1900. *The Real Estate Analyst* index moves similarly, with a one-year lead at both turns. Both indexes rise sharply after 1900, regaining their 1891 levels by 1904, and both continue to rise gradually until 1907. From 1907 to 1914 the movements are irregular, but both indexes are lower in 1914 than in 1907.

Our rent index is a simple average of indexes for six large cities, 1895–1914, and for five cities for 1890–95. The combined index is shown in Table 22 and the separate city indexes are shown in Table 32. The city indexes were computed from the rents asked in newspaper

TABLE 32
Rent Indexes for Six Cities, 1890–1914
(1914 = 100)

	New York	Chicago	Philadelphia	Boston	Cincinnati	St. Louis
1890	95	86	105	91	a	98
1891	94	88	100	86	a	104
1892	94	88	102	93	a	108
1893	94	91	102	92	a	106
1894	94	84	99	87	a	108
1895	95	80	98	91	82	97
1896	92	77	102	92	85	100
1897	93	72	98	88	82	97
1898	89	75	98	86	77	100
1899	90	74	96	87	83	91
1900	88	76	95	82	77	90
1901	86	74	96	88	83	93
1902	86	81	96	88	76	91
1903	92	79	96	84	86	108
1904	104	82	100	83	93	116
1905	106	81	102	88	91	116
1906	109	80	102	90	97	110
1907	106	84	107	92	105	116
1908	100	87	99	95	102	109
1909	98	87	100	96	97	103
1910	98	88	100	93	100	112
1911	98	88	101	100	101	95
1912	98	89	99	98	100	99
1913	98	95	96	103	103	105
1914	100	100	100	100	100	100

SOURCE: See text.
a The Cincinnati sample is too small to be used before 1895.

97

advertisements in one paper in each city in April and September of each year.[34] The papers used were the *New York World*, the *Chicago Tribune*, the *Philadelphia Press*,[35] the *Boston Globe*, the *Cincinnati Enquirer*, and the *St. Louis Post-Dispatch*. We used data for the last Sunday in April and September because these precede traditional moving days in many cities. When not enough observations were available on the last Sunday of the month, issues of preceding Sundays were also used.

The selection of cities was dictated by the availability of files or microfilms of newspapers and our cities are obviously not in any sense a representative sample of all cities.[36] We needed to find newspapers that advertised dwelling units at about the rent level paid by working-class families as shown in the various budget studies; several papers examined, including the *New York Times* and the *Boston Transcript*, advertised only, or primarily, dwelling units at much higher rent levels. We attempted to construct an index for Cleveland from advertisements in the *Cleveland Plain Dealer*, but discarded it because there were too few observations before 1905.

Within each city, we collected rent data for the sizes and kinds of dwelling units in which workers typically lived as shown by the 1918 budget-study data for families with incomes below $1,500. The rents for the various sizes and kinds of units were combined using the fixed 1918 weights shown in Table 33. These are derived from the number of budget-study families living in each size and type of unit. Classes whose weight was very small were omitted. Thus, we collected data only for houses in Philadelphia, and only for apartments in New York, Boston, and Chicago, but for both houses and apartments in Cincinnati[37] and St. Louis.

[34] For a previous use of data from classified advertising in newspapers to construct a price index, see Gregory C. Chow, *Demand for Automobiles in the United States*, Amsterdam, 1957.

[35] The Philadelphia data for September 1914 are from the *Ledger* rather than the *Press*; holdings of the *Press* at New York Public Library end in mid-1914. The level of the September index is 5 per cent above April. This is a slightly smaller rise than the rise from April to September in our index for New York, using data from the *World* in both months. We therefore conclude that the Philadelphia rise results from the outbreak of war in Europe rather than from the change in sources. In other cities we did not record the April and September observations separately.

[36] If we assume that the selection of cities by *The Real Estate Analyst* was not identical with ours, the similarity of our index with theirs can be taken as some evidence that our selection of cities does not strongly affect the behavior of our index. The dispersion among our city indexes offers some evidence to the contrary.

[37] For Cincinnati after 1900 we collected data on both apartments and unfurnished rooms in three- and four-room units. The average rents on the unfurnished rooms were

Apart from size, we had little control over the quality of housing. It was seldom possible to tell from the advertisements whether or not a unit had a bathroom, an inside toilet, or steam heat. Units advertised as having garages or stables or as being in buildings with elevators were excluded as being upper- or middle-class housing.

TABLE 33

Weights for City Rent Indexes, by Size and Type of Dwelling Unit

	New York	Chicago	Philadelphia	Boston	Cincinnati	St. Louis
Houses						
3-room[a]	—	—	—	—	8.9	11.8
4-room	—	—	17.1	—	9.5	23.5
5-room	—	—	29.7	—	6.1	6.7
6-room	—	—	45.1	—	—	—
7-room[b]	—	—	8.1	—	—	—
Apartments						
3-room[a]	24.9	—	—	9.5	61.2[c]	49.6
4-room	43.4	43.0	—	43.0	14.3[c]	8.4
5-room	27.6	31.6	—	37.5	—	—
6-room	4.1	25.4	—	10.0	—	—

SOURCE: *Cost of Living in the United States*, BLS Bulletin 357, pp. 276–333; housing data for families with income below $1,500.

[a] Includes all the weight of the budget-study class "less than 4 rooms."

[b] Includes all the weight of the budget-study class "more than 6 rooms."

[c] After 1900, series for these units include both "apartments for rent" and "unfurnished rooms for rent." See note 37.

However, units were never excluded solely because of high rent. In Chicago, many steam-heated units could be identified and these were excluded. When they are included, the average level of rents is far higher than that shown in budget studies for working-class families.[38]

Table 34 shows for selected years the number of observations on which the city rent indexes are based. With the exceptions mentioned

consistently lower for each size. We believe, therefore, that these were units lacking some facilities such as bathrooms or inside toilets (the 1918 budget study shows only 61 of 134 Cincinnati flats and apartments surveyed as having bathrooms and only 80 as having inside toilets). We combined apartments and unfurnished rooms for each size, giving apartments a constant weight of 29.4 per cent for the three-room units and 52.4 per cent for the four-room units. These weights for each size were obtained by dividing the total number of observations for apartments for 1900–1918 by the total number of observations for both types of units. The series for apartments only for 1895–1900 was linked to the combined series by a one-year overlap at 1900.

[38] A study of Chicago housing in 1909 states "modern steam-heated flats . . . are not as a rule occupied by working class families." Great Britain, Board of Trade, *Cost of Living in American Towns*, 1911, p. 144.

in the notes to this table, the samples are of generally satisfactory size. The weakest is Cincinnati before 1908; the small size of this sample probably explains the somewhat erratic movement of the Cincinnati index for 1895–1905.

Five of our city indexes were continued to 1918 to permit comparison of rent levels with the 1918 budget study. The Philadelphia index could not be continued to 1918 because the sample became too small. For 1914–18 we can compare our series with BLS rent indexes in

TABLE 34

Number of Observations Used in Constructing City Rent
Indexes, Selected Years, 1890–1914

	New York	Chicago	Philadelphia	Boston	Cincinnati	St. Louis
1890	620	217	179	142	a	199
1895	644	269	319	386	74	352
1900	748	271	273	460	129	233
1905	544	228	267b	466	91b	225b
1910	494	230	267	499	418	193
1914	967	217	303c	494	555	264

SOURCE: See text.

a The Cincinnati sample is too small to be used before 1895.

b Three of the city indexes are based on small numbers of observations during the rapid rise in rents of 1902–4. The lowest figures for each city are: Philadelphia, 71 observations for 1902; Cincinnati, 41 observations for 1902; and St. Louis, 37 observations in 1904. That little housing was for rent in St. Louis in 1904 was undoubtedly an effect of the Louisiana Purchase Exposition.

c The Philadelphia index for 1912 is based on only 56 observations for January and March. Holdings of the *Philadelphia Press* at the New York Public Library are incomplete for this year.

three cities (there were no BLS rent indexes for Cincinnati or for St. Louis before December 1917). These comparisons are shown in Table 35. In Boston and New York there is close agreement on the size of the rent rise from 1914 to 1918; the Chicago indexes diverge. Some of the differences in year-to-year movement may arise from the differences in timing between the two sets of indexes.

In general, our indexes are less stable than those of the BLS. This is because we measure rents asked for vacant units, while the BLS measures rents paid for occupied units under the terms of existing leases or arrangements. Clearly, the former is a more volatile measure, but there is little reason to expect the long-run trends of the two measures to diverge. Unless landlords overestimate what they can get for vacant units by more at some times than at others, each point on an index of rents paid should correspond to a weighted average of rents asked at previous times, where the weights are the percentages of all existing agreements entered into at each past time. Any constant percentage difference between rents asked at each date and those actually received under new agreements made at the same date would presumably disappear when the measures are converted to index numbers.

Both our indexes and the BLS indexes show little rise in rents during World War I, perhaps because the effects of rising incomes and costs were offset by the cutting off of immigration.

TABLE 35

Comparison of Rent Indexes, Three Cities, 1914–1918
(1914 = 100)

| | NBER Indexes (April and September) | | | BLS Indexes (December) | | |
	New York	Chicago	Boston	New York	Chicago	Boston
1914	100.0	100.0	100.0	100.0	100.0	100.0
1915	99.9	92.5	102.7	99.9	99.9	99.9
1916	98.2	91.8	98.2	99.9	100.7	100.1
1917	93.1	92.8	102.0	102.6	101.4	99.9
1918	105.3	96.9	102.2	106.5	102.6	102.8

SOURCE: NBER indexes: see text; BLS indexes: *Cost of Living in the United States*, BLS Bulletin 357, pp. 276–333.

In Table 36 the average levels of rents indicated by our newspaper data are compared with those shown by a number of budget studies and housing surveys. For the newspaper data, the average monthly rent for each size and type of unit is expressed in dollars per room, and these rents per room are weighted by the weights shown in Table 33. Where the survey data are given by room size, the same weights are used. Where they are given by income class, the weights are the number of persons in each class as shown by the survey itself. Descriptions of these surveys and our methods of using data from them are given in Appendix F. Table 37 expresses the comparisons of Table 36 in percentage terms.

On the whole, Tables 36 and 37 suggest that we have succeeded in collecting data representative of the rents paid by working-class families. The surveys for 1918, 1909, and 1907 were confined to such

101

TABLE 36

Comparison of Rent Levels by Cities, Selected Years, 1891–1918[a]
(average monthly rent per room)

Year and Sources	New York	Chi-cago	Phila-delphia	Boston	Cincin-nati	St. Louis
1891						
Boston Globe	b	b	b	$3.16	b	b
Massachusetts BLS	b	b	b	3.32	b	b
1893						
Newspaper data	$3.71	$3.41	$2.52	b	b	b
7th Special Report	4.09c	3.27	3.07	b	b	b
1900						
Chicago Tribune	b	2.89	b	b	b	b
City Homes Assn.	b	1.80	b	b	b	b
1902						
New York World	3.35	b	b	b	b	b
N.Y. Tenement Dept.	3.45	b	b	b	b	b
1907						
New York World	4.17	b	b	b	b	b
Chapin	3.86	b	b	b	b	b
1909						
Newspaper data	3.84d	3.27	2.48	3.49	$3.43d	$3.50d
British Board of Trade	3.83	2.71	2.81	3.08	3.63	3.82
1918						
Newspaper data	4.07	3.68	b	3.74	3.86	3.14
BLS Bulletin 357	3.79	3.21	b	3.15	3.46	3.83

[a] See Appendix F for discussion of sources and methods.
[b] Philadelphia newspaper data for 1918 were not usable. All other gaps in the table are due to lack of survey data for comparison.
[c] Manhattan only.
[d] To make size of units comparable with Board of Trade data, six-room units are omitted in New York and five-room houses are omitted in Cincinnati and St. Louis.

families; those of 1900 and 1895 were confined to slum areas. In only two cases does the newspaper rent level differ from the comparison level by more than 20 per cent. The largest difference appears in the Chicago comparison for 1900. The Chicago survey of 1900, however, was taken in three small districts with very bad housing conditions, the total area of which was only 221 acres.[39]

[39] City Homes Association, *Tenement Conditions in Chicago*, 1901, pp. 11–14 and 54.

The differences for 1918, a year of rising rents, are of the sort to be expected between rents paid under old arrangements and rents asked for vacant units. The difference in St. Louis is in the opposite direction from the others, which is consistent with the fact that our St. Louis rent index, unlike those for the other cities, falls from 1917 to 1918.

Since a constant percentage error in average rents would not affect the movement of our indexes, our chief interest in Tables 36 and 37 is in the trend of the percentage differences in the same cities.

Suppose we accept the premise that the surveys of actual rents paid are more comparable over time than, and therefore superior to, the

TABLE 37

Rent Levels from Newspaper Advertising as Percentages
of Rent Levels from Survey Data, 1891–1918
(per cent)

	New York	Chicago	Philadelphia	Boston	Cincinnati	St. Louis
1891				95		
1893	91	104	82			
1900		161				
1902	97					
1907	108					
1909	100	121	88	113	94	92
1918	107	115		119	112	82

SOURCE: Computed from data in Table 36, *q.v.*

series based on advertised rents asked. What kind of bias in our indexes would this suggest? In five of the six cities it would suggest that we overstate the rise in rents—either the survey rents rise less or fall more than advertised rents. This conclusion does not seem to depend on changes in the quality or nature of the survey data. The surveys of 1902, 1893, and 1891 are based on a larger number of dwelling units than later surveys. The 1902 and 1891 data are from complete censuses of rented units. They apply to families who, on the average, were probably higher in the income distribution than those surveyed in 1907 or 1909 or than those for which we have used the 1918 data. The 1893 survey, on the other hand, was of selected slum areas, and undoubtedly covered families who, on the average, were lower in the income distribution than the families surveyed from 1907 on.

103

Because our newspaper data are probably more nearly comparable over time than the surveys, the upward bias in our data suggested in the preceding paragraph may not really exist. There is, however, a different reason for believing that our rent index is biased upward: our failure to control for improvement in housing quality. Both our data and the survey data just discussed undoubtedly refer to better housing at the end of the period than at the beginning. The percentage of all units with bathrooms and inside toilets increased over the period, and the percentage in brick or stone buildings also may have increased. Except in Chicago, where we exclude steam-heated units, the percentage of all units with central heating also must have been rising. An index of rents for units of constant quality would, therefore, rise less than our index.

We have very little data on changes in housing quality during the period. For New York, we can compare data for 1907 and 1918. In 1907, Chapin found that 17 per cent of 318 working-class families with incomes between $600 and $1,099 had bathrooms.[40] The BLS data of 1918 covered 224 families with annual incomes below $1,500 living in flats and apartments, of which 40 per cent had bathrooms. The data on toilets do not appear to be comparable. Chapin gives data on private toilets, BLS on inside toilets, which may often have been shared. The difference in the proportion of families with bathrooms may, of course, represent one in coverage between the two samples rather than an improvement in sanitary facilities between 1907 and 1918. However, when we compare the average rents per room from these two studies, using the same income limits as those for the comparison of the percentage with bathrooms, we find a slightly higher average rent per room in the Chapin study (see Table 36).

For Boston, we can make comparisons of quality over a longer period. The complete census of rented dwelling units for 1891 shows 92 per cent of the families having toilets and 26 per cent having bathrooms.[41] In 1918, the BLS budget study found that 372 of 373 families surveyed lived in houses or apartments having toilets, and 206 (55 per cent) in houses or apartments having bathrooms. The average rent for Boston in 1918 from Bulletin 357, as shown in Table 36,

---

[40] Robert Coit Chapin, *The Standard of Living Among Working Men's Families in New York City*, 1907, p. 102.

[41] Massachusetts Bureau of Labor Statistics, *Twenty-third Annual Report*, 1893, pp. 116–125. Only 47 per cent of all families had private toilets.

applies to families living in apartments and having incomes below $1,500. Of the 224 families in this group, 223 lived in apartments having toilets (not necessarily private) and 114 (51 per cent) lived in apartments having bathrooms. Thus, the percentage of working-class families surveyed having bathrooms and toilets in 1918 was higher than the percentage of all tenants having such facilities in 1891.

It seems possible to explain the major movements of our rent index for all cities combined in terms of business conditions, immigration, and new construction. The fall from 1893 to 1900 is associated with the depression of the mid-1890's, during which there was a marked fall in the level of immigration. The slowness of rents to recover is characteristic of sticky prices. The rapid rise in rents from 1900 to 1907 coincides with the great increase in immigration during these years. Net arrivals of aliens (arrivals minus departures) were 385,000 in 1900, by far the highest figure since 1893.[42] From 1903 through 1907 they exceeded 500,000 each year and reached 767,000 in 1907. There was a lull in immigration during 1908, but by 1910 net arrivals exceeded the 1907 level. Why, then, does the rent index stop rising after 1907? The explanation seems to be that the number of new non-farm dwelling units started rose sharply in 1905 and stayed high for the next decade, even during the recession of 1908.[43] In short, from 1900 to 1907 construction lagged behind immigration and rents rose; from 1908 to 1914 immigration remained high but construction caught up and rents stabilized. This pattern of rents is unlike that of commodity prices, which continued to rise from 1907 to 1914.

Fuel and Light

Before 1907, Douglas uses the wholesale group index "fuel and lighting" as the basis for his retail index. After 1907, he uses the BLS indexes of the retail prices of coal and manufactured gas. The resulting index is unsatisfactory in several respects. It omits gas before 1907 and kerosene after 1907. Before 1907 it includes crude petroleum.

---

[42] See Simon Kuznets and Ernest Rubin, *Immigration and the Foreign Born*, Occasional Paper 46, New York, NBER, 1954.

[43] See David M. Blank, *The Volume of Residential Construction, 1889–1950*, Technical Paper 9, New York, NBER, 1954, p. 67. By citing the increase in the construction of nonfarm dwelling units, we do not mean to imply that many of the new units must have been occupied by immigrants or workers. As middle-class families move into new dwellings, working-class families may move into the units they vacate, and this process can relieve the pressure on rental levels for old units.

Moreover, the BLS retail index for gas after 1907 contains an error, which will be discussed below.

Our fuel and lighting index includes four fuels throughout: manufactured gas, bituminous coal, anthracite coal, and kerosene. To construct an index of the prices of manufactured gas we first corrected the BLS index for 1907–14. The original BLS index is based on data for a varying number of cities, decreasing from 37 in 1907 to 35 in 1912 and then increasing to 44 in 1913 and 1914. The gas prices for all cities were averaged in each year and index numbers were computed from these averages. However, all of the cities that were added in 1913 had rates higher than the average of the original group, so that this procedure makes the index understate the decline in prices. In correcting the index, we also used the BLS data for all cities. We computed the simple average of the percentage change in rates for illuminating gas in identical cities from April 15 to April 15 for each pair of years, and linked these averages.

The uncorrected BLS index is shown in the first column of Table 38; it has been computed from the average prices of gas shown in *Retail Prices*, 1890–1924, BLS Bulletin 396, October 1925, p. 222. (The BLS computed its index from these same average prices, but on the base 1913 = 100.) Our corrected index from the BLS data is given in the second column. Both indexes refer to the price of the first 1,000 cubic feet of gas per month. Where there was more than one gas company serving a city, the simple averages of rates by companies are used in both indexes.

To obtain data for the period before 1907, we wrote to a number of gas companies in large cities, asking for the domestic rates charged by them or their predecessors during 1890–1907. Usable replies were received from eight companies covering the following periods and cities: 1890–1907, New York, Chicago, Philadelphia, Cleveland, Baltimore, and Cincinnati; 1898–1907, Milwaukee and St. Louis.[44] The index shown in the third column of Table 38 is the simple average of the relatives for these cities, linked when the number of cities changes. For years containing a price change, the relatives are based on an average for the year, in which each rate is weighted by the

[44] The companies furnishing rate information were the Consolidated Edison Company of New York, the Peoples Gas, Light, and Coke Company (Chicago), the Philadelphia Gas Works (a division of the United Gas Improvement Company), the East Ohio Gas Company (Cleveland), the Baltimore Gas and Electric Company, the Cincinnati Gas and Electric Company, the Milwaukee Gas Light Company, and the Laclede Gas Company (St. Louis).

106

TABLE 38

Price Indexes of Manufactured Gas,[a] 1890–1914

(1914 = 100)

	BLS Uncorrected	BLS Corrected	Eight Cities[b]	Final (NBER)
1890			149.1	147.0
1891			147.4	145.3
1892			143.8	141.7
1893			145.8	143.7
1894			133.7	131.8
1895			132.7	130.8
1896			131.6	129.7
1897			130.6	128.7
1898			130.6	128.7
1899			125.3	123.5
1900			122.0	120.3
1901			119.4	117.7
1902			119.4	117.7
1903			119.4	117.7
1904			119.0	117.3
1905			118.2	116.5
1906			114.9	113.3
1907	105.3	109.8	111.4	109.8
1908	105.3	109.2	111.4	109.2
1909	104.3	108.3	108.0	108.3
1910	103.2	106.1	108.0	106.1
1911	101.1	103.8	102.8	103.8
1912	98.9	103.0	101.8	103.0
1913	101.1	102.1	101.8	102.1
1914	100.0	100.0	100.0	100.0

SOURCE: Uncorrected BLS index: *Retail Prices, 1890–1924*, BLS Bulletin 396, October 1925, p. 222; all other indexes: see text and note 43, below.

[a] Prices for first 1,000 cubic feet per month for illumination.

[b] Seven cities after 1909; six cities before 1898.

length of time it was in effect. For the two cities that had different rates for gas for illumination and for "general use" we have used the rate for illumination.

To permit a comparison of our index from company data with the BLS index, we have continued our index to 1914. Data for the companies included in the earlier segment were taken from the BLS bulletins. Cincinnati is dropped after 1908, since only natural gas was supplied beginning July 1909. Because our index is based on a much smaller number of observations, it is not as smooth as the corrected BLS index. However, there is a close correspondence in the trends. Our final index for gas is formed by linking the index for eight cities to the corrected BLS index at 1907.

For two reasons, our index understates the fall in gas prices paid by working-class families. First, we have not included natural gas, for lack of proper weights and sufficient information on the dates at which it was introduced. By 1914, natural gas was used in nine of the forty-nine cities covered by BLS reports, but in four of these some manufactured gas was also used. The rates per cubic foot for natural gas were much lower than those for manufactured gas, and its heat content was higher. The transition from manufactured to natural gas in a city thus represented a sharp drop in the cost of fuel.[45] The cheapness of natural gas led to its use in place of other fuels in cities where it was available. The 1918 budget study shows that in several of the cities served by natural gas the consumption of gas in thousands of cubic feet was two to four times the national average for families in the same income groups; in heat units the difference would be even larger.

The failure to account for block rates is a second, though less important, reason why our index understates the fall in gas prices. The index measures the rate for the first 1,000 cubic feet per month, though by 1918 the national average consumption for families with incomes below $1,500 was about twice this amount. At some time during our period, block rates were introduced in many cities, giving a lower rate per 1,000 cubic feet for quantities beyond some minimum amount. The introduction of block rates in the range from 1,000 cubic feet to the maximum quantities consumed by working-class families is an additional reduction in price not shown by our index. Block rates for domestic customers are unimportant for the eight sample cities before 1907; they appear only in Milwaukee for 1904–7. We do not have any data on block rates by cities for 1907–14.[46]

---

[45] For example, in Cincinnati in 1907 the rate for manufactured gas was 75 cents per 1,000 cubic feet for lighting and 50 cents per 1,000 cubic feet for fuel; this gas had approximately 600 btu. per cubic foot. Natural gas was introduced beginning in 1907 at 30 cents per 1,000 cubic feet, and had 1,130 btu. per cubic foot.

[46] The BLS later recomputed its index for 1907–14 on the basis of 3,000 cubic feet per month (*Retail Prices, 1890–1928*, BLS Bulletin 495, August 1929, p. 208). This index falls slightly faster than the index based on 1,000 cubic feet for 1907–11, but the difference is eliminated when the number of cities changes in 1912.

108

The movement of our gas index can be roughly checked by comparing it with data from the *Census of Manufactures*. This comparison is shown in Table 39. The census data are for average revenue per 1,000 cubic feet in all uses. Our data are derived from the index shown in the last column of Table 38 multiplied by 94 cents, the average price per 1,000 cubic feet in cities covered by the BLS in 1914. We have assumed no change in prices from 1889 to 1890 on the basis of data for two of the cities. The census figures fall somewhat more rapidly than ours, especially between 1889 and 1899. This undoubtedly reflects growing industrial and commercial use of gas at rates

TABLE 39

Comparison of Prices of Manufactured Gas,
Census Years, 1889–1914
(dollars per 1,000 cubic feet)

	NBER[a]	Census of Manufactures[b]
1889	1.38	1.42
1899	1.16	1.03
1904	1.10	1.00
1909	1.02	0.92
1914	0.94	0.86

SOURCE: NBER series: see text and note 44. Census series: *Census of Manufactures, 1914*, Vol. II, p. 544.

[a] Price of first 1,000 cubic feet for domestic use—NBER price index of manufactured gas, shown in last column of Table 38, multiplied by 94 cents, the average price per 1,000 cubic feet in cities covered by the BLS in 1914.

[b] Average revenue per 1,000 cubic feet in all uses.

below domestic rates and also, perhaps, the introduction of block rates in domestic use. The effect on the level of the census series of including commercial and industrial uses is partly offset by the including of small cities, where rates were generally higher than in the large cities covered by the BLS surveys.

The first three columns of Table 40 show the remaining components of our fuel index. The two coal indexes are the BLS retail indexes beginning in 1907. To these have been linked simple averages of price relatives taken from the wholesale price index for 1890–1907. For bituminous coal, we have used the relatives for Pittsburgh (Youghiogheny) bituminous at Cincinnati, and Georges Creek semibituminous,

TABLE 40

Fuel and Light Price Indexes, 1890–1914

(1914 = 100)

| | Coal | | Kerosene | Fuel and Light | |
	Bituminous	Anthracite		NBER[a]	Douglas[b]
1890	84	68	101	83	65
1891	92	71	89	85	61
1892	88	77	80	84	63
1893	89	78	74	84	60
1894	79	67	74	76	59
1895	78	58	93	78	66
1896	74	70	105	83	77
1897	71	74	91	80	68
1898	66	70	92	78	64
1899	72	68	89	79	73
1900	88	73	107	91	80
1901	89	81	102	92	79
1902	108	85	98	100	88
1903	122	92	118	112	108
1904	98	92	125	105	93
1905	95	92	112	101	88
1906	94	93	114	101	92
1907	98	92	114	101	95
1908	97	93	112	101	95
1909	94	93	112	100	95
1910	95	94	106	99	95
1911	96	94	86	95	95
1912	96	97	103	99	97
1913	100	101	108	102	99
1914	100	100	100	100	100

[a] A weighted average of the first three columns of this table and the last column of Table 38 (see text for underlying sources and methods).

[b] Converted to the base 1914 = 100, from Paul H. Douglas, *Real Wages in the United States, 1890–1926*, Boston, 1930, p. 38.

f.o.b., New York Harbor. The series for Georges Creek at the mine was not used; it includes no transportation, which makes up more than half the price of the same coal at New York. For anthracite, we used the series for chestnut, egg, and stove sizes. The series for broken anthracite was not used, since this is less suitable for use in stoves and home furnaces than sized coal.

Here and in our other uses of wholesale prices, we have not adopted Douglas's device of adjusting the data to a presumed retail basis. This

110

adjustment, as mentioned previously, is based on the differences in movement between wholesale and retail price indexes for an identical group of foods. We have no confidence that the differences between these indexes for a commodity as unlike food as coal would be at all similar. The adjustment seems as likely to introduce error as to remove it.

The index for kerosene for 1898–1914 is based on retail prices taken from the reports of the New Jersey Bureau of Industrial Statistics; to this series we have linked the wholesale price of refined petroleum, 150° fire test, water-white for 1890–98. After 1898, these two series are very similar.

We have been unable to find any price series for wood used for fuel in the period. Electricity was of negligible importance in working-class homes before World War I. The wholesale price series for matches was not used for lack of weights; expenditures on them must have been very small.

The weighting of the fuel index is made complicated by the tremendous growth in the importance of gas over the period. To use 1918 weights throughout would greatly overstate the importance of changes in gas prices early in the period, while to use 1890 weights throughout would underweight gas at the end of the period. No data were available that permitted us to derive weights for any intermediate date. We have used, therefore, varying weights obtained by computing percentage weights for 1890 and 1918 and making linear interpolations for intervening years. This is the only point in our cost-of-living index where constant weights have not been used.

The weights for 1890 and 1918 are shown in Table 41. The 1918

TABLE 41

Weights for the Fuel and Light Price Index, 1890 and 1918
(per cent)

| | Coal | | Kerosene | Gas |
	Bituminous	Anthracite		
1890	42.91	33.66	22.17	1.26
1918	30.57	23.98	19.78	25.67

SOURCE: 1890 based on *Cost of Production: Iron, Steel, Coal, Etc., Sixth Annual Report of the Commissioner of Labor*, 1891, and *Cost of Production: The Textiles and Glass, Seventh Annual Report of the Commissioner of Labor*, 1892; 1918 based on *Cost of Living in the United States*, BLS Bulletin No. 357, p. 391.

111

weights are derived from the expenditures on fuel and light of families with incomes below $1,500 as shown in Bulletin 357. The expenditures are shown separately for families living in houses and in apartments, in the following categories: bituminous coal, anthracite coal, wood, gas, electricity, and "all other." We omit wood and electricity and give the weight of "all other" to kerosene. For each category, we computed for houses and apartments separately the simple average expenditure of the three income classes "under $900," "$900 and under $1,200," and "$1,200 and under $1,500." We converted these averages into two percentage distributions by categories and combined the distributions, using as weights the number of families with incomes below $1,500 living in houses and in apartments.

The weights for 1890 are derived from the *Sixth* and *Seventh Annual Reports of the Commissioner of Labor*. These reports show budgets by individual families for a considerable number of families in each of several industries. By omitting two high-wage industries, we get a group where the average income of husbands is close to that of all manufacturing workers.[47] The individual family budgets show expenditures on fuel and light separately and specify, in most cases, what kind was used. From this information we have computed the average expenditure per family on gas, coal, and kerosene. Coal was the predominant fuel and kerosene the main source of light, but small amounts of gas were used for both purposes. Expenditures on wood, frequently used for fuel, were omitted in computing our weights. Since these reports do not distinguish between bituminous and anthracite coal, we allocate the weight of coal to the two varieties in 1890 in the proportions shown by the 1918 study.

Our final price index for fuel and light is compared with Douglas's index in the last two columns of Table 40. Both become more stable after 1907, when they are based wholly on retail prices. The sharp peak in the Douglas index in 1903, resulting from a rise in the wholesale price of bituminous coal, is somewhat less pronounced in our index. The former rises considerably more than ours before 1903. The inclusion of crude petroleum in Douglas's and of gas in ours seems to be the principal source of this difference. It seems probable that a better index would rise still less than ours. The use of wholesale prices before 1907 undoubtedly biases our index upward, and the biases in our gas index work in the same direction. However, the omission of wood, the price of which probably rose relative to the

47 See p. 78.

prices of other fuels, may work in the opposite direction. Wood accounted for roughly 18 per cent of expenditures on fuel in 1890 and roughly 11 per cent in 1918 for families with incomes below $1,500.

Other Components of the Index

Two components of our index remain to be discussed: liquor and tobacco, and all other items. For liquor and tobacco we have only the wholesale prices of three items: plug tobacco, smoking tobacco, and proof spirits. Unfortunately, we have no data before 1913 for finished whiskey or for beer, which probably accounted for most of workingmen's expenditures on liquor. Douglas[48] has combined the three available series into an index which we have used. This index gives the combined wholesale prices before Douglas's adjustment to a presumed retail basis; that is, it is not his "most probable index of the retail price of spirits and tobacco."[49]

The expenditures represented by "all other items" are very diverse. The bulk of them are for services, of which medical care and insurance are the most important. In the 1918 budgets of families in the income class $900–1,200, these accounted for two-fifths of the total. Other important expenditures for services included those for carfare, amusement, and laundry sent out. Commodities account for about one-sixth of the total. Of these, cleaning supplies, soap, and toilet articles are most important, and newspapers next.

A wholesale price series is available for laundry starch beginning in 1890, but there is none for laundry soap until 1913. It might have been possible for us to collect data from primary sources on carfares and the prices of newspapers, but in view of the small importance of these expenditures, it did not seem worthwhile. Therefore, we have not constructed any price index for "all other items."

Douglas implicitly assumes that the prices of unpriced items (rent and sundries) move with the average price of all priced items. Because of the peculiar composition of our unpriced items, in particular their heavy weighting with services, we have assumed, instead, that their prices moved with the price of all priced items other than food.[50]

---

[48] *Real Wages*, p. 609.

[49] *Ibid.*, p. 38.

[50] This is the same assumption made by Ethel D. Hoover in her new consumer's price index for 1860–80, though items outside the groups represented by some prices are much less important in her index than in ours (see "Retail Prices after 1850," *Trends in the American Economy in the Nineteenth Century*, Princeton University Press for NBER, 1960).

(About 40 per cent of the weight of all priced nonfoods in our index is given to rent, a payment for services.)

Weighting the Components

Of the three available budget studies (1890, 1901, and 1918), the 1901 study is the most suitable for deriving weights for the components of our index, because it lies roughly in the middle of the period we cover. Within this study, two different sets of family budgets could be used. The first set, used by Douglas and by the National Industrial Conference Board, is the set of 11,156 "normal families." A normal family as the term is used in the *Eighteenth Annual Report of the Commissioner of Labor*,[51] is one having a husband at work, a wife, not more than five children, none over 14 years of age, and no dependent, boarder, lodger, or servant; and having expenditures for rent, lighting, fuel, food, clothing, and sundries. The second possible set is that of all 25,440 families studied. (For this set, we must use the housing expenditures of tenants only, because we have no data on the movement of the costs of home ownership.) Neither Douglas nor the NICB states any reason for preferring to use the normal families. The percentage distribution of expenditures for the two sets is shown in Table 42, lines 1 and 3.

TABLE 42
Weights for the Cost-of-Living Index, 1901 Data
(per cent)

	Food	Cloth-ing	Home Furnish-ings[a]	Rent	Fuel and Light	Liquor and Tobacco[a]	All Other
Normal families	43.1	13.0	3.4	18.1	5.7	3.0	13.7
Douglas, implicit weights	63.2	19.1	5.0	0.0	8.4	4.4	0.0
All families	44.1	13.4	3.4	16.7[b]	5.4	3.0	14.0
NBER implicit weights	44.1	17.9	4.5	22.3	7.2	4.0	0.0

SOURCE: Lines 1 and 3 are from *Eighteenth Annual Report of the Commissioner of Labor*, pp. 367, 505, 509, and 593; line 2 is derived from line 1 and Paul H. Douglas, *Real Wages in the United States, 1890–1926*, Boston, 1930; line 4 is derived from line 3 (see text).
a The expenditures on home furnishings and on liquor and tobacco are based in all cases on the budgets of 2,567 families who reported detailed expenditures.
b Housing expenditures based only on families in rented housing.
51 *Report*, p. 18.

114

We have used the budgets for all families for three reasons: (1) the definition of normal families seems artificially restrictive and lowers the average size of these families; (2) the all-families sample is larger; (3) we estimate that the average income of husbands in normal families was slightly above that in all families, and the average income of husbands in both sets was substantially above the average annual earnings of all manufacturing workers.[52]

The differences between the two distributions of expenditures are not large; on the average, all families spent slightly more on food and clothing and less on rent and fuel than did normal families. These differences seem to arise from the smaller size of normal families, which, in turn, results from the upper limit on the age of children and the exclusion of families having dependent relatives. The average size of normal families is 3.96 persons, of all families, 4.88 persons. Food and clothing claim more of the budget in large families, leaving less for other expenditures.[53]

The largest differences between the expenditure patterns of normal families and all families are for rent and food. Our rent index rises less than most components of our total index and the food index rises more. Given the direction of the differences in expenditure patterns, this means that the use of weights based on normal families would cause our index to rise slightly less than it does.

The major differences between our weights and Douglas's are not those just discussed, but those arising from the assumptions about the prices in the sectors for which there are no price data. The assumption that the cost of unpriced items moves with that of certain priced ones is, in effect, a redistribution of weights, resulting in a new set of implicit weights for the priced items. Line 2 of Table 42 shows the implicit distribution of weights in the Douglas index after the weights for the unpriced groups, rent and all other items, are redistributed among the priced sectors in proportion to their original weight (line 2 of Table 42 is derived from the normal-family weights of line 1). Line 4 of Table 42 shows the implicit weights for our index after the weight of all other items is redistributed to the remaining nonfood

---

[52] The income from all sources of all families was above that of normal families because the normal families had no income from boarders and lodgers or the earnings of grown children.

[53] See *Eighteenth Annual Report*, pp. 584–585 for tables showing percentage distributions of expenditures in normal families by income class and family size. These show, within income classes as family size rises, a quite consistent fall in the share of rent in all expenditures and a rise in the shares of food and clothing.

115

sectors in proportion to their original weights (line 4 is derived from the all-family weights of line 3).

Because we have a rent component in our index and Douglas does not, our implicit weights are lower than his for every other sector. However, the only major difference is for food. This difference occurs because Douglas lets food share the weight of his unpriced items and we do not. Our explicit weight for food is one percentage point higher than his, yet food has 63 per cent of the total weight of his index, and only 44 per cent of the total weight of ours.

The Cost-of-Living Index as a Whole

Table 43 and Chart 7 compare two cost-of-living indexes, Douglas's and ours, and the wholesale price index. The major difference between the first two is in the extent of their rise over the full period. The Douglas index rises by one-third, ours by one-tenth. In general, ours moves later, reflecting the inclusion of sluggish rents and the use of fewer wholesale price series. The Douglas index falls from 1890 to 1894, while ours does not fall until 1893, the year in which the depression of the 1890's began. However, the fall in our index is much sharper and longer. The Douglas index begins to rise again 1896, ours not until 1900. After 1900, the movements are similar, though those of the Douglas index are all more pronounced. Our index does not reflect the recession of 1904 until 1905, and it continues to move downward from 1908 to 1909.

In comparing these indexes with the wholesale price index, two points may be noted. First, our index rises less than the wholesale price index over the full period, while Douglas's rises more. Second, Douglas's tends to lead the wholesale price index at turns (1896–97, 1904–5) while ours lags or coincides. The latter would seem to be the normal relationship between a wholesale and a consumer price index. The very heavy weight of food in the Douglas index undoubtedly accounts for these features of its relationships to the wholesale price index.

In closing the discussion of our cost-of-living index, we may examine briefly the way in which it should be interpreted. In the BLS Consumer Price Index, the weights are quantities consumed in an initial base year. Thus, it tells us how much it would cost today to buy the basket of commodities typically consumed in the base period. As is well known, such an index rises more than an index with

TABLE 43

Comparison of Cost-of-Living and Wholesale
Price Indexes, 1890–1914
(1914=100)

| | Cost-of-Living | | Wholesale |
	NBER	Douglas	Price
1890	91	75	81
1891	91	73	82
1892	91	73	76
1893	90	72	77
1894	86	70	69
1895	84	70	70
1896	84	72	66
1897	83	72	67
1898	83	72	69
1899	83	74	74
1900	84	76	80
1901	85	78	79
1902	86	80	85
1903	88	84	85
1904	89	83	86
1905	88	83	85
1906	90	86	88
1907	94	91	94
1908	92	87	91
1909	91	87	97
1910	95	92	99
1911	95	95	95
1912	97	96	101
1913	99	99	100
1914	100	100	100

SOURCE: NBER: see text; Douglas: Paul H. Douglas, *Real Wages in the United States, 1890–1926*, Boston, 1930. Wholesale prices: *Wholesale Prices, 1890–1919*, BLS Bulletin 269, July 1920, p. 15.

given-year quantity weights because consumers tend to buy more of the things whose prices rise least or fall most.

No such simple interpretation can be given to our index, which uses a mixed system of weights determined by the availability of data rather than by any index-number theory. Our clothing, home furnishings, and rent indexes have fixed expenditure weights with a 1918 base—that is, a base after the end of the period with which we deal. In the case of expenditure-weighted arithmetic averages of price

117

relatives, no general statement can be made about the bias arising from the choice of a date for the weighting base in the absence of knowledge of the relevant elasticities of demand. The fuel index uses shifting weights based on 1890 and 1918 expenditures; these weights do not create any weighting bias that can be simply stated. For the food index and the weighting of the major groups, fixed 1901 weights

CHART 7

Comparison of Cost-of-Living and Wholesale Price Indexes, 1890–1914

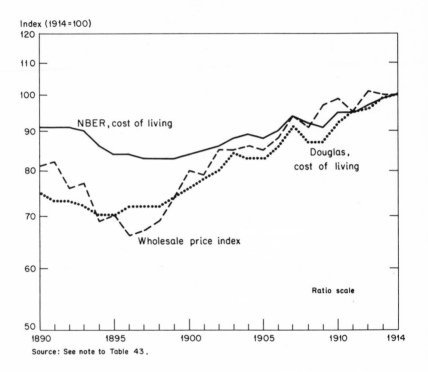

Index (1914=100)

Source: See note to Table 43.

are used. The system of weights as a whole probably produces an index with less of an upward bias than a Laspeyres index, and perhaps one with a downward bias compared to some "ideal" index, but we cannot be sure.

The biases resulting from weighting are probably much less important than those in the measurement of prices. Here again, there are offsetting considerations. There are large differences in movement

118

between our series for clothing and home furnishings and comparable wholesale series. Some of these arise from differences in the items covered and in the timing of the introduction of new items. However, it is possible that these components have a downward bias of unknown origin. On the other hand, the rent index is undoubtedly biased upward by the failure to control for improvement in the quality of housing, and the fuel index is biased upward by the use of wholesale prices for coal until 1907 and by the omission of natural gas.

Our cost-of-living index in general is certainly less accurate than official indexes for more recent periods. However, the offsetting considerations just discussed do not seem to suggest a clear bias in either direction.

CHAPTER 5

Real Wages

THIS chapter deals with our estimates of real wages, i.e. the money-wage series of Chapter 3 divided by the cost-of-living index of Chapter 4. Table 44 and Chart 8 present our series for real wages for

TABLE 44

Real Earnings in All Manufacturing, 1890–1914

	REAL EARNINGS, NBER (1914 DOLLARS)		INDEXES OF REAL EARNINGS (1914=100)			
			NBER		Douglas	
	Hourly	Daily	Hourly	Daily	Hourly	Weekly
1890	$0.158	$1.58	72	77	93	101
1891	0.158	1.58	72	77	97	105
1892	0.160	1.60	72	78	97	105
1893	0.168	1.68	76	82	99	107
1894	0.162	1.61	74	79	100	107
1895	0.165	1.64	75	80	100	107
1896	0.172	1.72	78	84	100	107
1897	0.168	1.67	76	82	98	106
1898	0.166	1.66	75	81	98	106
1899	0.176	1.75	80	86	99	106
1900	0.179	1.77	81	87	99	106
1901	0.185	1.82	84	89	98	105
1902	0.191	1.87	87	91	99	105
1903	0.193	1.88	88	92	98	103
1904	0.190	1.84	86	90	99	104
1905	0.194	1.88	88	92	101	105
1906	0.204	1.96	93	96	101	105
1907	0.203	1.95	92	95	99	103
1908	0.201	1.92	91	94	100	103
1909	0.203	1.94	92	95	101	103
1910	0.209	1.99	95	97	98	101
1911	0.213	2.01	96	98	96	98
1912	0.213	2.00	97	98	100	101
1913	0.224	2.09	102	102	101	101
1914	0.220	2.04	100	100	100	100

SOURCE: Tables 10 and 22 and Paul H. Douglas, *Real Wages in the United States, 1890–1926*, Boston, 1930, pp. 108 and 130.

120

all manufacturing, and compare them with the Douglas series. Our index of daily earnings is directly comparable with Douglas's index of full-time weekly earnings, since we regard all changes in the length of the full-time workweek as changes in hours per day.

The total rise in real hourly earnings from 1890 to 1914 shown by our series is 40 per cent, compared with a rise of 8 per cent in Douglas's. While the Douglas series reaches its 1914 level by 1894, ours

CHART 8

Comparison of Indexes of Real Earnings, 1890–1914

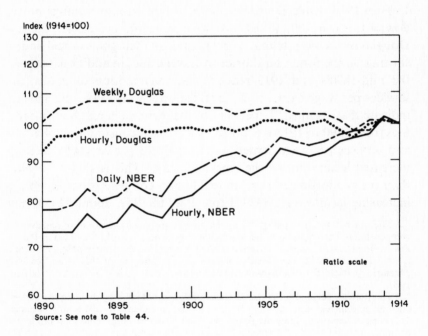

Index (1914=100)

Source: See note to Table 44.

rises throughout the period; it is never below its previous peak for more than three years.

Our real-wage index has a clear tendency to fall in cyclical contractions, though it leads the contraction of 1908 by a year. The small year-to-year movement of the Douglas series often seems random, but it has some tendency to rise in cyclical contractions. This difference arises largely from the inclusion of union rates in the Douglas money-wage series. When the two components of the Douglas series

121

are examined separately, it is seen that real hourly earnings in payroll industries fall in cyclical contractions while real hourly earnings in union industries rise.

The downward cyclical flexibility of real hourly earnings from 1890 to 1914 is in marked contrast to more recent experience. Since 1929, real average hourly compensation (earnings plus wage supplements) in manufacturing has fallen in only three years—from 1931 to 1932 and from 1944 to 1946. The fall from 1945 to 1946 occurred during a business expansion. There was no decline in 1929–31, 1938, 1949, or 1954.[1]

Our index of real daily earnings rises more or less steadily from 1890 to 1913, while Douglas's index of real weekly earnings moves downward from 1893 to 1913. As we have mentioned earlier, the two Douglas series indicate that workers took all their gains in real hourly earnings in the form of a shorter workweek and, in addition, between the mid-1890's and 1913 reduced the consumption of goods and services per wage earner to get a still shorter workweek. Our indexes indicate that, at most, 77 per cent of the increase in real hourly earnings from 1890 to 1913 was taken as increased consumption of goods and services per wage earner, and at least 23 per cent was taken in increased leisure during the working years.[2] This is slightly smaller than the proportion of gains in real hourly compensation devoted to increasing leisure since 1929. From 1929 to 1957, about 32 per cent

[1] The statements in this paragraph are based on estimates by one of us of real average compensation (earnings plus wage supplements) per hour of work, presented in *Wages, Prices, Profits, and Productivity*, Report of the Fifteenth American Assembly, 1959. For a technical description of the money compensation component of this series, see *New Measures of Wage-Earner Compensation in Manufacturing, 1914–57*, New York, NBER, 1960.

[2] The portion devoted to increased consumption is obtained by dividing the percentage increase in real daily earnings by the percentage increase in real hourly earnings. This is equivalent to dividing the actual increase in daily earnings (consumption) by the potential increase, where the potential increase is the increase in hourly earnings times the average daily hours at the initial date. The comparison ends with 1913 so that both starting and ending years will be cyclical peaks, since the final percentages are sensitive to small changes in the increase in earnings, and hourly earnings were depressed during the recession of 1914.

The figures shown in the text reflect only the shortening of the full-time workweek and do not allow for increases in the number of holidays or vacations, paid or unpaid. This is the reason for the words "at most" and "at least" in the text. Possible increases in holidays or vacations might be taken into account by comparing the rise in real hourly earnings with that in real annual earnings. On this basis, 36 per cent of the gain in earnings was used to increase leisure. However, some of the decrease in the number of days in operation per year from 1890 to 1913 could represent slack demand in 1913 (the cyclical peak in business activity on a quarterly basis was reached in the first quarter). Thus, the most that can be said is that the percentage of the increase in real wages used to increase leisure was between 23 and 36.

122

of the gains in real hourly compensation was used to increase leisure.[3] On the assumption that there have been no important changes in the demand function for leisure, the rough similarity of these percentages for the two periods tends to support our estimates of real wages.

Table 45 presents our series on real hourly earnings by industry. We find increases in real hourly earnings in every industry from 1890 to 1914, and these increases range in size from 16 per cent in the leather industry to 56 per cent in paper and paper products. The two industries with the smallest increases, leather and dyeing and finishing textiles, were industries in which there was relatively little growth in employment. However, for the group as a whole there is no significant correlation between increase in employment and increase in real wages.

Our finding that real hourly earnings rose in all the industries studied again differs from Douglas's findings. He found a fall in real hourly earnings from 1890 to 1914 in two of six union industries and three of eight payroll industries. In the extreme case, slaughtering and meat packing, real hourly earnings fell 14 per cent. Table 46 compares the changes for the industries common to the two studies.

The rise in real average hourly earnings within industries as shown in Table 45 is usually not as steady as the rise for all manufacturing. In most industries, a peak is reached in 1893 or 1894 that is not regained for a number of years. In dyeing and finishing textiles, real earnings are below the 1893 level until 1906. A more typical case is all textiles, which regains its 1893 level in 1903. The intervening decade includes the depression of the 1890's and the initial years of heavy immigration. The industries with only brief breaks in the rise of real earnings after 1893 are wool, where the 1893 peak is regained in 1896, and iron and steel, where it is regained in 1898. In iron and steel there is a new peak in 1902 that is not regained until 1909.

To compare our data on real wages with productivity data, we have extended the real-wage series backward one year, using Long's data. The comparison is made for 1889–1913 so as to eliminate the effect on all the series of the recession of 1914. We find that the annual rate of increase in real hourly earnings over the period is 1.3 per cent, which is the same as that of output per weighted unit of labor and capital combined for the private domestic economy, as estimated by

---

[3] Based on the estimates cited in note 1. The increase in leisure for this period includes increases in vacations and holidays.

TABLE 45
Real Hourly Earnings in Fourteen Manufacturing Industries, 1890–1914
(1914 dollars)

	Cotton	Wool	Silk	Hosiery and Knit Goods	Dyeing and Finishing Textiles	All Textiles	Boots and Shoes	Leather	Electrical Machinery	Paper and Paper Products	Rubber	Glass	Foundries and Machine Shops	Iron and Steel
1890	0.109	0.127	0.132	0.103	0.169	0.116	0.176	0.186		0.131	0.173		0.203	
1891	0.108	0.129	0.134	0.106	0.172	0.117	0.174	0.192		0.130	0.170		0.207	
1892	0.108	0.131	0.129	0.111	0.171	0.118	0.178	0.190		0.134	0.168		0.204	0.187
1893	0.116	0.147	0.147	0.118	0.186	0.129	0.182	0.190		0.138	0.181		0.208	0.191
1894	0.121	0.136	0.143	0.120	0.189	0.128	0.187	0.185		0.144	0.179		0.216	0.184
1895	0.114	0.140	0.134	0.118	0.183	0.125	0.184	0.192	0.196	0.142	0.181		0.215	0.182
1896	0.116	0.147	0.147	0.120	0.189	0.129	0.179	0.194	0.198	0.145	0.191		0.213	0.189
1897	0.117	0.145	0.138	0.115	0.181	0.127	0.177	0.193	0.211	0.143	0.188		0.208	0.185
1898	0.110	0.149	0.136	0.116	0.183	0.126	0.172	0.187	0.208	0.136	0.192		0.212	0.192
1899	0.111	0.150	0.138	0.123	0.179	0.128	0.175	0.183	0.208	0.148	0.191	0.219	0.209	0.217
1900	0.118	0.155	0.129	0.121	0.177	0.131	0.175	0.181	0.206	0.151	0.186	0.231	0.213	0.222
1901	0.119	0.154	0.127	0.120	0.175	0.131	0.177	0.180	0.214	0.152	0.191	0.239	0.214	0.230
1902	0.121	0.156	0.135	0.120	0.182	0.135	0.178	0.179	0.216	0.158	0.185	0.243	0.225	0.235
1903	0.124	0.158	0.140	0.125	0.178	0.138	0.188	0.179	0.233	0.151	0.183	0.226	0.229	0.230
1904	0.120	0.154	0.135	0.121	0.174	0.133	0.183	0.182	0.220	0.159	0.184	0.241	0.225	0.216
1905	0.116	0.157	0.147	0.127	0.186	0.134	0.194	0.180	0.224	0.160	0.188	0.254	0.228	0.219
1906	0.121	0.165	0.143	0.141	0.186	0.140	0.194	0.191	0.228	0.158	0.200	0.244	0.236	0.225
1907	0.132	0.164	0.146	0.131	0.177	0.142	0.197	0.190	0.222	0.169	0.191	0.242	0.233	0.229
1908	0.132	0.169	0.136	0.133	0.183	0.144	0.201	0.195	0.229	0.193	0.214	0.256	0.239	0.233
1909	0.130	0.171	0.151	0.136	0.190	0.146	0.201	0.200	0.228	0.183	0.214	0.245	0.241	0.241
1910	0.137	0.170	0.151	0.138	0.190	0.149	0.205	0.198	0.233	0.183	0.220	0.253	0.243	0.245
1911	0.137	0.169	0.158	0.139	0.184	0.150	0.208	0.204	0.235	0.190	0.220	0.257	0.246	0.260
1912	0.140	0.176	0.160	0.144	0.187	0.155	0.210	0.195	0.242	0.195	0.224	0.257	0.248	0.255
1913	0.142	0.175	0.181	0.147	0.194	0.161	0.212	0.226	0.244	0.197	0.225	0.265	0.254	0.277
1914	0.141	0.190	0.169	0.160	0.201	0.160	0.212	0.214	0.240	0.205	0.239	0.263	0.253	0.266

Kendrick.[4] The rate of increase in output per production-worker man-hour in manufacturing over the same period was 2.1 per cent.[5] The fact that output per man-hour in manufacturing rose more than the real hourly earnings of production workers implies that the wage earner's share of manufacturing output declined. This inference is supported by Solow's more direct study of the wage earner's share of value added in manufacturing.[6] A falling share for wage earners probably means a rising share for capital, and this might be thought

TABLE 46

Changes in Real Average Hourly
Earnings, by Industry, 1890–1914
(per cent)

	NBER	Douglas
Cotton	+30	+18
Wool	+50	+12
Hosiery and knit goods	+55	+14
Boots and shoes	+20	+8
Iron and steel[a]	+42	−2
Foundries and machine shops	+25	−4[b]

SOURCE: Table 45 and Paul H. Douglas, *Real Wages in the United States, 1890–1926*, Boston, 1930, pp. 98 and 104.
[a] 1892–1914.
[b] Union rate data for metal trades.

to support the conclusion of Hansen and Rubinow that the lag of wages behind prices had increased profits. However, we have found no such lag.

Although this study cannot investigate the causes of changes in relative shares in manufacturing income, it may be appropriate to point out that factor proportions were changing in the same direction as relative shares. Kendrick has reported a sharp rise in capital-output ratios in manufacturing during the period. One plausible interpretation of the rising share of capital is therefore that this larger share was needed to cover the costs of using more capital and to sustain the

[4] See John W. Kendrick, *Productivity Trends in the United States* (to be published by Princeton University Press for the NBER).

[5] This estimate is based on Kendrick's index of manufacturing output, Fabricant's estimates of production worker employment in manufacturing, and the series on days in operation and average daily hours presented in this study. The man-hours are thus identical with those underlying the estimates of average hourly earnings.

[6] Robert M. Solow, "The Constancy of Relative Shares," *American Economic Review*, September 1958, p. 627.

inflow of capital to the manufacturing sector over a long period. This is, however, not the only possible interpretation.[7]

What, then, of the idea that immigration held down real wages during the period? The finding of an increase in real wages in no way denies the importance of immigration. We have seen that the wave of heavy immigration that began in 1900 coincided with a sharp rise in our rent index, and that during this wave our real wage measures for a number of industries remained below their previous peaks for several years. In a larger sense, immigration was probably an important factor in keeping both the rate of increase in real wages and in productivity during this period below the rates achieved more recently.[8]

It is, of course, reasonable that the assimilation of the massive immigration of 1900–1914 should retard the growth of real wages. Not only were the new immigrants less skilled, on the whole, than the native born, but the shift in the sources of immigration from northern and western Europe to southern and eastern Europe meant that they were, on the whole, less skilled and less literate than were the new immigrants of earlier periods. But, in reckoning productivity, so long as we measure labor inputs in man-hours and not in units of constant quality, these arguments suggest a retardation in the growth of productivity as much as in real wages. There undoubtedly were individual cases in which employers took advantage of the ignorance of immigrants to pay them less than their worth, but such cases could hardly drive a huge wedge between the movements of productivity and real wages for a large sector of the economy.

We conclude that the accepted view that real wages did not rise in the quarter century before World War I is largely the product of faulty statistics. Since our measures of money wages differ from previous ones principally in level and very little in movement, the fault in the earlier indexes of real wages lies largely on the cost-of-living side.

[7] We are grateful to Zvi Griliches for persuading us to modify an earlier, more dogmatic version of this passage. This does not imply his agreement with the present version.

It has been assumed in the text that supplies of factors to a sector of the economy are quite elastic over long periods so that the effects on income shares of changes in factor proportions are not fully offset by opposite shifts in factor prices. If factors receive their marginal products, this amounts to assuming that the production function for a sector over a long period is not a fixed Cobb-Douglas function.

[8] For 1929–57, one of us has estimated the increase in real hourly compensation of manufacturing wage earners at 3.5 per cent a year and the increase in output per production-worker man-hour in manufacturing at 2.7 per cent a year. See *Wages, Prices, Profits, and Productivity*, p. 24.

126

This study has not examined real wage statistics for any country except the United States. However, since the cost-of-living indexes for the United Kingdom before World War I have the same kinds of defects as the accepted indexes for the United States, it might well be worth while to re-examine also the conclusion that real wages in the United Kingdom were unchanged from 1890 to 1913.

Appendixes

APPENDIX A

Sources and Characteristics of State Earnings Data

THE period covered by our study was the period of greatest activity of state bureaus of labor statistics. This activity was largely inspired by one man, Carroll D. Wright. Wright headed the Massachusetts Bureau of Statistics of Labor, the first in the country, from 1873 to 1885, and was the first United States Commissioner of Labor, 1885–1905. The patterns he set in Massachusetts were followed by many of the other states, as is apparent from the notes that follow. Wright was also instrumental in organizing an association of officials of bureaus of labor statistics which was active during this period and helped to provide uniformity among the statistics of some of the states.

After World War I, as the statistical services of the federal government improved, the statistical activities of the states tended to decline, and many of the series used here were discontinued. Even during our period, though almost every state issued some labor statistics, there were great variations in quality from state to state. In some states, frequent changes in personnel or administrative arrangements produced frequent shifts in the kinds of data collected and gaps in many of the series. For several states, however, especially Massachusetts and New Jersey, we were impressed with the continuity and full coverage of the data, the detail in which they were presented, and the care that seemed to have been exercised in compiling them.

Massachusetts[1]

Massachusetts is the only state whose data cover our entire period. The information provided is consistent throughout. For all industries combined, and for separate industries, the data include the number of establishments, the average number of wage earners, total wages paid, and average days in operation per establishment. Beginning in 1908, the industry classification used is identical with that of the census. The data for 1909 and 1914 are identical with the census data,

[1] SOURCE: Massachusetts, Bureau of Statistics, *Annual Report on the Statistics of Manufactures*, Nos. 6–29, 1890–1914.

131

but provide, in addition, the number of days in operation. There are no omissions of industries or employees.

Before 1908 the industry classification is not identical with that of the census but is rather similar, and there were a few difficulties in combining series into census industries. The coverage of census employment is not complete, but is generally very high. Through 1905, two sets of data are provided for each year, one covering the same establishments included in the preceding year, one covering the establishments included in the following year. The two differ very little. We have consistently used the second, which generally covers more employees because of the entry of new firms.

New Jersey[2]

The New Jersey data are consistent from 1895 to 1914 and provide the same information as the Massachusetts data. Industry definitions are consistent throughout but do not correspond with census definitions, being generally finer in industries important in the state. After 1899, coverage of employment is generally very high. Before that time the coverage is incomplete, and we have made little use of the data for individual industries.

Pennsylvania[3]

The Pennsylvania data consist of a number of distinct segments, which will be discussed in turn. With exceptions to be mentioned, they provide the same information as the Massachusetts data. In all segments, the industry classification does not correspond to the census and is very much finer in industries important in the state.

For 1892–1905 the data consist of series for two sets of identical establishments, one covering 1892–1901, the second covering 1896–1905. Here, and in Appendix C, we shall refer to these as the "1892 series" and the "1896 series." In general, the 1896 series has greater coverage. The coverage of both series is usually a rather small fraction of census employment. However, the use of identical establishments removes the principal difficulty we find in series with incomplete coverage—erratic movement resulting from changes in coverage from year to year.

2 SOURCE: New Jersey, Bureau of Statistics of Labor and Industries, *Annual Reports*, Nos. 18–37, 1895–1914.

3 SOURCES: Pennsylvania, Bureau of Industrial Statistics, *Annual Reports*, Vols. 20–40, 1892–1912; Pennsylvania, Department of Labor and Industry, *Annual Reports*, Vols. 1–2, 1913–1914.

We have no way of knowing whether some of the same establishments are included in both series during the period of overlap. We have, therefore, not averaged the two to avoid double-counting some establishments. Our all-manufacturing series uses the 1896 series for 1896–1901 and links the 1892 series to it for 1892–95. In our industry series we have chosen between the two sets of data for the overlap period on the basis of the number of employees covered and the correspondence of annual earnings with the Census in 1899. Where simple acceptance of both series at the dates of transition (1895–96 or 1901–2) produced a movement similar to that of the continuous series, we have used this method. Elsewhere, we have linked the two series to remove differences in level.

From 1905 to 1912 the coverage of the Pennsylvania data increases greatly and becomes almost complete. The data no longer relate to identical establishments. For some industries sharp changes in coverage or industry definition within the period 1905–12 prevent us from accepting the series.

In 1913, the work of collecting statistics of manufactures was transferred from the Bureau of Industrial Statistics in the Department of Internal Affairs to the Bureau of Statistics and Information in the Department of Labor and Industry. This transfer produced serious discontinuities in the statistics. There were often sharp changes in the number of employees reported, and apparently in industry definition, which were not always reflected in industry titles. The resulting erratic movement of many earnings series led us to reject them. Where Pennsylvania series for 1913–14 were accepted, we had to deal with a special problem. The data for 1913 do not give the number of salaried employees and wage earners separately, although they do give salaries and wage payments separately. We have either assumed that the ratio of wage earners to all employees was the same in 1913 as in 1914, or, in some cases, we have estimated the number of salaried workers in 1913 by making a linear interpolation of average annual earnings of salaried workers from 1912 to 1914 and dividing the 1913 figure into salaries paid.

Ohio[4]

The Ohio data are very different in form from those of the other states we have used. The data consist of the number of workers employed, average number of days worked, average daily earnings,

[4] SOURCE: Ohio, Bureau of Labor Statistics, *Annual Reports*, Nos. 18–37, 1893–1912.

and average yearly earnings *by occupations* within industries, separately for Cincinnati, Cleveland, Columbus, Dayton, Toledo, other
cities, and villages. No averages whatever are provided for these
many observations for occupations. Within industries we have computed employment-weighted averages of daily wages for all occupations and localities combined. These become our interpolating
series. For census years only, we have computed similar employment-
weighted averages of days worked to be used in estimating average
daily earnings from census data. These estimates of daily earnings
serve as benchmarks for the interpolating series.

The industry definitions of the Ohio data are consistent throughout,
though they do not correspond exactly to census definitions. The
coverage of the data is very good after 1900 but often low before that
time, so that we have had to reject the early portions of some Ohio
series.

Wisconsin[5]

The Wisconsin statistics are, in general, similar to those of Massachusetts. However, the series are interrupted by a three-year gap,
for 1900, 1901, and 1902, resulting from a fire in the State House that
destroyed the records of the Bureau of Labor and Industrial Statistics.
The industry classifications are consistent throughout and, for the
series we have used, seem to be similar to census definitions. Prior to
1896, there are data for weeks in operation rather than days in operation; we have converted these to days by multiplying them by six.
There are also no employment data before 1896, so that Wisconsin is
excluded from the 1889 estimates of coverage of census employment
in Appendix C, although we use some Wisconsin data back to 1890.

Connecticut[6]

The Connecticut data are also similar to the Massachusetts, but
cover only five years, 1900–1904. They are on a fiscal-year basis, with
years ending June 30. We have converted them to a calendar-year
basis by averaging adjacent years. We thus lose one year's observations, and the data appear in some of our series for the four years
1900–1903. Nevertheless, the employment covered by the Connecticut
series is included in the employment covered by our series for 1899

[5] SOURCE: Wisconsin, Bureau of Labor and Industrial Statistics, *Biennial Reports*,
Nos. 4–9 and 11–13, 1889–99 and 1903–7.
[6] SOURCE: Connecticut, Bureau of Labor Statistics, *Annual Reports*, 1900–1904.

and 1904 in the coverage tables of Appendix C. The Connecticut industry definitions did not present any special problems.

Rhode Island[7]

The Rhode Island data are similar to the Massachusetts, though they cover only the textile industries for 1893–1903. Two sets of data are presented for each year, one comparable with the preceding year and one with the following. In each pair, we have used the data with the largest coverage. The days in operation per year are given separately by establishments; we have computed employment-weighted averages. In the woolen industry some establishments are reported as operating more than 312 days per year, in some cases more than 365 days; the highest figure is 588. All entries of more than 312 days are marked "running overtime." We have assumed that this refers to two-shift operations and that the number of shifts operated was counted. In computing average days in operation, we have entered all establishments "running overtime" as operating 312 days.

The industry titles are unchanged during the period and correspond to census industries.

Maine[8]

The Maine data are for two industries only, cotton and woolen mills. They are for fiscal years ending June 30, for 1895–1903. We have averaged adjacent years and the data appear in our series for 1895–1902. The time in operation is presented in weeks, which we have converted to days by multiplying by six. The data on time in operation are for individual establishments, and we have computed employment-weighted averages.

South Carolina[9]

The South Carolina data include average employment, total wages, and average days in operation. We have used only one series, textiles, which is described in Appendix B under cotton.

[7] SOURCE: Rhode Island, Bureau of Industrial Statistics, *Annual Reports*, Nos. 8–18, 1893–1903.

[8] SOURCE: Maine, Bureau of Industrial and Labor Statistics, *Annual Reports*, 1895–1903.

[9] SOURCE: South Carolina, Department of Agriculture, Commerce, and Industries, Labor Division, *Annual Reports*, Nos. 1–6, 1909–14.

Other States

A number of other states published some data on employment and earnings during 1890–1914. In one case, Missouri, we made extensive attempts to use the data and discarded them because of rapidly shifting coverage, which produced very erratic wage series. The other data were rejected at the outset. For several western states, the data covered too few workers to have an appreciable effect on any of our series. In two cases, West Virginia and Washington, the data were available only for every second year. New Hampshire data provided the number of days in operation for 1893–98 only, a period that does not include a census benchmark. Virginia data provided days in operation only as establishment-weighted averages. Illinois and Indiana had data only for a few scattered years. The remaining states omitted some essential item from the data, either number of employees or number of days in operation.

APPENDIX B

Definitions of Industries and List of State Series Used

THE industries for which wage series are provided in the text are defined below in terms of census industries as of 1914. In some cases, they are differently defined in earlier censuses; the 1914 census provides explanations of such differences.

Cotton

Census industry: cotton manufactures (includes cotton goods, cotton smallwares, and cotton lace).

Massachusetts—cotton goods, 1890–1914; cotton smallwares, 1908–14.

Pennsylvania—1892 series used 1892–1901: tapestries and table-cloths, cotton yarns, cotton goods, chenille goods. The 1896 series used 1901–5: cotton yarns, cotton goods, chenille goods, lace goods. Other series used were: towels, 1910–14; curtains, 1910–12; cotton goods, 1906–14; lace goods and draperies, 1906–14. (For 1906–10, the last two series are given separately for Philadelphia and the rest of the state.)

Connecticut—cotton mills, cotton goods, 1900–1903 (cotton goods include batts, thread and yarn, rope, cord, twine, netting, and webbing, which are products included in the census industry, plus a few items, such as laundered shirts, that are not included).

Rhode Island—cotton goods, 1893–1903.

Maine—cotton mills, 1895–1903.

South Carolina—textiles, 1910–14. This series covered 166 establishments in 1914, of which twelve did not produce cotton textiles. Seven produced hosiery; one each produced asbestos textiles, wool and cotton blankets, hair cloth, and jute bagging; and one did bleaching and finishing.

Wool

Census industry: wool manufactures except carpets and rugs (includes woolen goods, worsted goods, felt goods, and wool hats).

137

Massachusetts—woolen goods, 1890–1910; worsted goods, 1890–1910; woolen and worsted goods, 1910–14; wool hats, 1909–12; felt goods, 1908–14.

New Jersey—woolen and worsted goods, 1898–1914.

Pennsylvania—1892 series used 1892–96: worsted goods, worsted yarns, woolen goods, woolen yarns. The 1896 series used 1896–1905: woolen and worsted fabrics; woolen and worsted cassimeres; worsted, woolen, and cotton yarns; upholstery goods; woolen blankets, flannels, etc.; woolen and worsted yarns; and wool hats. Other series used were: woolens and worsteds, Philadelphia, 1906–9; woolens and worsteds, blankets and flannels, outside Philadelphia, 1906–9; woolen goods, 1910–12; cotton and woolen yarns, Philadelphia, 1907–9; yarns, 1910–12; upholstery and drapery goods, Philadelphia, 1906–9; upholstery goods, 1910–12; blankets and flannels, 1910–12.

Connecticut—woolen mills, 1900–1903.

Rhode Island—woolen goods, 1893–1903.

Maine—woolen mills, 1895–1902.

Silk

Census industry: silk goods, including throwsters.

Massachusetts—silk and silk goods, 1890–1914.

New Jersey—silk, broad and ribbon; silk throwing; silk dyeing, 1896–1914 (some of the establishments included in silk dyeing are probably in the census industry "dyeing and finishing of textiles").

Pennsylvania—1892 series used 1892–96: silk broad goods; 1896 series used 1896–1905: silk broad goods and ribbons; silk—broad goods, thrown silk, yarns, etc., and ribbons. Other series used were silk dress goods and throwing, 1906–9; silk ribbons, dress goods, and throwing, 1906–9; silk throwing, 1906–9; silk, 1910–14.

Connecticut—silk goods, 1900–1903.

Rhode Island—silk goods, 1896–1903.

Hosiery and Knit Goods

Census industry: hosiery and knit goods.

Massachusetts—hosiery and knit goods, 1890–1914.

New Jersey—knit goods, 1898–1914.

Pennsylvania—1892 series used 1892–96: hosiery; hosiery and knit goods; knit goods. The 1896 series used 1896–1905: hosiery;

knit goods, underwear. Other series used were hosiery, 1906–12; knit goods, 1906–12 (for 1906–9, given separately in and outside of Philadelphia).

Wisconsin—knitting works, 1890–99 and 1903–7.
Connecticut—hosiery and knit goods, 1900–1903.
Rhode Island—hosiery and knit goods, 1893–1903.

Dyeing and Finishing Textiles

Census industry: dyeing and finishing textiles exclusive of that done in textile mills.

Massachusetts—print works, dye works, and bleacheries, 1890–1907; dyeing and finishing textiles, 1908–14.

New Jersey—dyeing and finishing cotton goods, 1898–1914.

Pennsylvania—dyers, bleachers, and finishers, 1906–12; dyeing and finishing textiles, 1913–14.

Rhode Island—print works, dye works, and bleacheries, 1893–1903.

All Textiles

Census industries: This is a combination of the census industries included in the five preceding series, plus two additional industries: carpets and rugs other than rag; and cordage, twine, jute, and linen goods. It excludes the manufacture of clothing and of such miscellaneous textile products as awnings, bags, belting, etc., and also excludes several related industries such as wool shoddy, haircloth, fur-felt hats, and mats and matting.

In computing this series, we have combined the component series for all industries by states and then combined the states using census employment weights. The list below gives the states series, *in addition to those listed in the five component industries above*, used in the "all textiles" series. Wisconsin, which is included in hosiery and knit goods, was not used in computing all textiles.

Massachusetts—carpetings, 1890–1907; carpets and rugs other than rag, 1908–14; cordage and twine, 1890–1914; mixed textiles, 1890–96; cotton, woolen, and other textiles, 1890–95.

New Jersey—cotton goods, 1899–1914 (not included in our series on the cotton industry because of poor correspondence with census industry); thread, 1899–1914; carpets, 1898–1914.

Pennsylvania—1892 series used 1892–96: carpets, mixed textiles,

139

cotton and woolen goods, miscellaneous yarns. The 1896 series used 1896–1905: carpets, cotton and woolen cloths, carpet yarns. Other series used were cordage and twine, 1906–14; carpets, 1906–14 (given separately in and outside Philadelphia, 1906–9); woolen, worsted, felt goods, and wool hats, 1913–14; hosiery and knit goods, 1913–14. (The last two series were omitted from their respective industry series because of sharp changes in employment and earnings in 1913–14. These changes seem to result from misclassifying some establishments by industry in 1913. When these series are combined with others in all textiles, the movement of both earnings and employment is reasonable.)

Boots and Shoes

Census industries: boots and shoes, not including rubber boots and shoes; boot and shoe cut stock, exclusive of that produced in boot and shoe factories; boot and shoe findings, exclusive of those produced in boot and shoe factories.

Massachusetts—boots and shoes, 1890–1914 (1890–1907 includes boots and shoes, factory product; soles, heels and cut stock; boot and shoe findings; stitching, heeling, etc.); boot and shoe findings, 1908–11; boot and shoe cut stock, 1908–11; boot and shoe cut stock and findings, 1912–14.

New Jersey—shoes, 1890–1914.

Pennsylvania—men's, women's, misses', and children's shoes, 1896–1905 (1896 series) and 1906–9; boots and shoes, 1910–14.

Ohio—boots and shoes, 1893–1912.

Wisconsin—boots and shoes, 1890–99 and 1903–7.

Leather

Census industry: leather, tanned, curried, and finished.

Massachusetts—leather, 1890–1907; leather, tanned, curried, and finished, 1908–14.

New Jersey—leather, 1899–1914.

Pennsylvania—leather, miscellaneous, 1906–12; shoe leather, enameled and glazed kid, 1906–12; sole and harness leather, 1906–9; sole leather, 1910–12; harness leather, 1910–12; tanneries, 1910–12.

Wisconsin—tanners and curriers, 1890–95; leather, 1896–99 and 1904–7.

Electrical Machinery

Census industry: electrical machinery, apparatus, and supplies.

Massachusetts—electrical apparatus and appliances, 1896–1907; electrical machinery, apparatus, and supplies, 1907–14.

New Jersey—electrical appliances, 1898–1914; lamps (light bulbs), 1898–1914; gas and electric fixtures, 1902–14.

Pennsylvania—electrical supplies, 1896–1905 (1896 series); electrical apparatus and lamps, 1906–9; electrical supplies, 1910–14; fixtures, gas and electric, 1912–14. (There is a separate census industry "gas and electric fixtures," but it had fewer than half as many employees in Pennsylvania, according to the 1914 Census, as are covered by this state series.)

Ohio—electrical goods and supplies, 1896–1912.

Paper and Paper Products

Census industries: paper and wood pulp; bags, paper not made in paper mills; boxes, fancy and paper; labels and tags; paper patterns; card cutting and designing; cardboard, not made in paper mills; envelopes; paper goods, n.e.s.

Massachusetts—paper and paper goods, 1890–95; paper, 1896–1907; paper boxes, 1897–1907; paper goods, n.e.s., 1896–1914; paper and wood pulp, 1908–14; envelopes, 1909–14; boxes, fancy and paper, 1908–14.

New Jersey—paper, 1898–1914; boxes, wood and paper, 1898–1912 (over two-thirds of employment in wood and paper boxes combined in 1913 is in paper boxes); boxes, paper, 1913–14.

Pennsylvania—1896 series used 1896–1905: paper manufactories; paper, paper boxes, envelopes, etc.

Wisconsin—paper and pulp, 1890–99, 1903–7.

Connecticut—paper goods, 1900–1903.

Rubber

Census industry: rubber goods (includes rubber belting and hose, rubber boots and shoes, and rubber goods, n.e.s.).

Massachusetts—rubber and elastic goods, 1890–1908; boots and shoes, rubber, 1908–14; rubber goods, n.e.s., 1909–14.

New Jersey—rubber goods (hard and soft), 1898–1914.

Ohio—rubber goods, 1900–1910.

Connecticut—rubber goods, 1900–1903.

141

Glass

Census industries: glass; glass cutting, staining, and ornamenting.

New Jersey—glass, window and bottle, 1899–1914; glass, cut tableware, 1908–14.

Pennsylvania—1896 series used 1899–1905: window glass, bottles, and table goods. Other series were glass, window, 1908–14; glass bottles, 1908–14; glass, plate, 1908–14; glass, decorative, 1910–14; lamps and chimneys, 1910–14; glass, tableware, 1910–14; glass, cut, 1910–14; glass, stained, 1910–12.

Ohio—glass and glassware, 1901–12.

Foundries and Machine Shops

Census industries: engines, steam, gas, and water; foundry and machine shop products; gas machines and gas and water meters; hardware; iron and steel—cast-iron pipe; locomotives not made by railroad companies; plumbers' supplies, n.e.s.; pumps, steam, and other power; steam fittings and steam and hot-water heating apparatus; stoves and hot-air furnaces; stoves, gas and oil; structural ironwork not made in steel works or rolling mills. (This list, except for the two stove industries and locomotives, makes up the industry "foundry and machine shop products" as used in the data by states of the Census of 1909. Stoves and hot-air furnaces and locomotives were included in foundry and machine shop products in the Censuses of 1889 and 1899. Stoves, gas and oil, were combined with stoves and hot-air furnaces in the data by states of the Census of 1909.)

Massachusetts—machines and machinery; cooking, lighting, and heating apparatus, 1890–1907; foundry and machine-shop products, hardware, steam fittings and heating apparatus, stoves and hot-air furnaces, structural ironwork not made in steel works or rolling mills, 1908–14.

New Jersey—boilers, tanks, etc.; foundry (iron); furnaces, ranges and heaters; machinery; steel and iron, structural, 1899–1914. (The Census of 1914 shows no structural shapes produced in rolling mills in New Jersey in 1914, and only one rolling mill producing structural shapes in 1909. The state series "iron and steel, structural," covers twenty-three establishments in 1909.)

Pennsylvania—1892 series used 1892–96: iron foundries and machine works; stoves, ranges, heaters, etc.; hardware; engines and boilers; boilers; bridges; locomotives and engines; car couplers. The

142

1896 series used 1896–1905: iron and steel bridges; stoves, ranges, and heaters; bath boilers, tanks, etc.; hardware specialties; cast-iron pipe; building and structural ironwork; engines, boilers, etc.; iron vessels and engines; boilers, tanks, stacks, etc.; machinery; foundries and machine shops; locomotives, stationary engines, etc.; plumbers' supplies; steam pumps; iron fences and rails. Other series were machinery and castings, 1906–7; iron and steel bridges and structural work; gas, gasoline, and steam engines and oil well supplies; locomotives, stationary engines, and metallic packing; hardware specialties 1906–9; foundries and machine shops, 1908–9; structural iron; iron and steel bridges; gas and gasoline engines; foundries; machinery; machine tools; stoves, heaters, and ranges; gas meters; boilers, tanks, and vats; castings; engines and boilers; plumbers' supplies; pumps and valves; radiators and steam fittings; ventilators, elevators, and fire escapes, 1910–12.

Ohio—boilers, engines, and tanks; foundry and machine shop products; machinery; stoves, ranges, and furnaces, 1893–1912; iron (structural and architectural), 1894–1912.

Connecticut—general hardware, iron and iron foundries, machine shops, 1900–1903.

Iron and Steel

Census industries: blast furnaces; steel works and rolling mills; tin plate and terne plate.

Massachusetts—iron and steel: steel works and rolling mills, 1909–14.

New Jersey—pig iron, 1899–1913; steel and iron (bar), 1899–1914.

Pennsylvania—1892 series used 1892–96: pig iron; malleable iron; steel; iron and steel sheets and plates; plate and bar; rolling mills, general products; nails and spikes. The 1896 series used 1896–1905: pig iron; steel plants and rolling mills that make a rolled product; steel mills that do not roll or finish their product; tin plate, black plate works. Other series used were pig iron; iron and steel, ingots and castings; iron and steel, rolled; tin and terne plate, 1906–12. The following series are used in 1914 only (affecting only weighted days in operation for 1914): iron, pig, basic foundry and forge; ferro-alloys; bars, rolled iron; bars, muck iron; ingots, crucible; castings, steel; billets, blooms, and slabs, steel; bars, rolled steel; plates, universal; plates, sheared; plates, black for tinning; rails; shapes, structural, heavy; shapes, structural, light; shapes, other iron and steel;

143

sheets; tin plate; rods, steel in coils; pipes and tubing, rolled; hoops, bands, and cotton ties; bolts, nuts, and rivets; nails and spikes, cut and wrought; wire nails; axles; horse shoes (the last five series include some establishments other than rolling mills, but such establishments include less than half the employment covered by the series in each case).

Ohio—steel, iron, and tin, 1901–12.

APPENDIX C

Establishment and Employment Coverage of State Earnings Data, by Industry, Census Years, 1889–1914

TABLE C–1

	Establishments		Wage Earners		Number of Wage Earners per Establishment	
	Number	% of Census	Thousands	% of Census	State Data	Census Data
Silk						
1889a	10	2.1	2.4	4.8	235	105
1899b	198	41.0	41.0	62.7	207	135
1904b	305	48.9	43.4	54.5	142	128
1909	411	48.2	68.0	68.6	165	116
1914	523	58.0	74.5	68.8	142	120
Hosiery and knit goods						
1889a	33	4.0	3.7	6.2	113	73
1899b	140	13.9	23.9	28.6	171	83
1904b	124	10.8	25.2	24.2	203	91
1909	451	32.8	51.7	40.0	115	94
1914	102	6.3	14.3	9.5	140	93
Dyeing and finishing textiles						
1889a	21	8.5	4.3	22.1	207	79
1899	83	27.9	14.2	47.8	171	100
1904	59	16.4	10.0	28.1	169	99
1909	129	30.3	16.1	36.5	124	103
1914	242	47.7	20.7	42.6	85	96
All textiles						
1889a	417	9.1	112.9	21.8	271	113
1899b	1,243	26.1	324.8	49.1	261	139
1904b	1,156	22.8	287.3	38.8	248	146
1909	1,973	41.7	439.7	50.1	223	185
1914	2,224	45.2	454.1	49.2	204	188

(continued)

NOTE: For cotton, wool, and boots and shoes, see Table 7 and accompanying text. For notes to a and b see p. 146.

TABLE C-1 (continued)

	Establishments		Wage Earners		Number of Wage Earners per Establishment	
	Number	% of Census	Thousands	% of Census	State Data	Census Data
Leather						
1889a	145	8.1	6.0	17.3	41	19
1899	176	13.5	13.2	25.3	75	40
1904	190	18.1	16.3	28.4	86	55
1909	286	31.1	26.6	42.8	93	68
1914	208	28.1	16.4	29.4	79	75
Electrical machinery						
1899	67	11.5	15.2	36.3	227	72
1904	158	20.2	26.7	44.2	169	77
1909	218	21.6	39.4	45.1	181	86
1914	269	26.1	37.2	31.5	138	115
Paper and paper products						
1889a	84	5.6	7.8	13.8	92	38
1899b	361	18.9	27.8	30.6	77	48
1904b	385	18.5	31.9	26.9	83	57
1909	340	14.2	27.3	19.2	80	59
1914	340	14.0	43.1	26.4	127	67
Rubber						
1889a	28	16.8	6.5	32.3	232	121
1899b	93	30.9	19.0	51.9	204	121
1904b	125	47.2	27.9	63.6	223	166
1909	110	41.2	28.8	58.5	262	184
1914	109	31.9	22.4	30.3	206	216
Glass						
1899	38	4.9	13.6	23.5c	357	75
1904	84	9.9	25.6	35.4c	305	85
1909	191	20.2	42.5	54.4c	223	83
1914	232	23.6	32.9	39.9c	142	84

a Massachusetts establishments and employment only. Additional states are included in the wage series beginning in 1892 or 1893. Wisconsin wage series for 1889–95 do not have corresponding data on employment and number of establishments.

b Includes the number of establishments and employment in Connecticut for the fiscal year including half of the year shown; wage series includes Connecticut for the calendar years 1900–1903.

c Based on census employment as given in the census, without adjustment for seasonality.

TABLE C-1 (concluded)

	Establishments		Wage Earners		Number of Wage Earners per Establishment	
	Number	% of Census	Thousands	% of Census	State Data	Census Data
Foundry and machine shops						
1889a	214	2.7	15.5	5.4	73	36
1899b	1,164	10.6	145.4	34.1	125	39
1904b	1,777	15.9	197.3	39.6	111	45
1909	2,066	15.0	184.2	31.8	89	42
1914	1,111	7.8	75.7	12.5	68	42
Iron and steel						
1899	—d	—d	102.9	45.5	—d	312
1904	—d	—d	164.9	66.6	—d	386
1909	391	57.1	204.4	72.0	523	414
1914e	319	51.6	157.9	55.7	495	458

d Not available. Number of Pennsylvania establishments (state data) not given in source.

e Includes Pennsylvania establishments and employment. The Pennsylvania data for 1914 were used only to compute the average number of days in operation. State earnings data for 1913 exclude Pennsylvania and cover only 5,400 workers. Coverage for 1910–12 is comparable to 1909.

APPENDIX D—List of Items in the Price Indexes for Home Furnishings and Clothing

TABLE D-1
Home Furnishings

Item No.	Description and Major Changes	Unit	1918 Price	Average Expenditure per Article, 1918[a]		Series Begins	Ward Data End	Number of Links[b]	1918 Sears Catalogue	
				Low	Average				Number	Page
1a	Carpet, part wool	yard	$0.92	$0.86	$1.41	1890	1896	3	37N1040	1146
1b	Carpet, all wool Brussels, 27 in.	yard	1.39	0.80	0.96	1890	1897	3	37N1004	1146
2	Linoleum, printed	sq. yd.	0.82			1890	1897	4	37N2142	1150
3a	Chair, hardwood dining	one	1.98	1.92	3.90	1890	1896	5	1N25	1038
3b	Chair, reed rocker	one	3.65			1890	1897	2	1N904	1050
4a	Table, dropleaf, hardwood	one	6.85	7.34	11.82	1890	1897	2	1N2404	1085
4b	Table, extension, solid oak	one	11.75			1890	1898	3	1N2410 1/3	1085
5a	Couch (bed lounge, 1890–95)	one	14.50	16.18	23.65	1890	1901	7	1N512 1/3	1056
5b	Couch	one	21.75			1902	none	3	1N536 1/3	1056
6a	Chiffonier, oak, 5-drawer	one	7.45	7.92	15.45	1895	1902	2	1N4708 1/3	1119
6b	Dresser, hardwood, with mirror	one	15.45			1890	1901	3	1N433 1/3	1115
7a	China closet	one	15.95			1901	none	2	1N2710 1/3	1089
7b	Sideboard, hardwood with mirror	one	21.45	16.64	23.89	1890	1898	3	1N2618 1/3	1088
8a	Bedstead, hardwood	one	6.95	6.72	11.07	1890	1897	5	1N5108	1123
8b	Bedstead, metal	one	8.65			1892	1898	4	1N5346	1127
9a	Bedsprings	one	{4.48	3.69	6.24	1901	1896	4	1N5759	1129
9b			6.88}				none	none	1N5765	1129
10a	Mattress, excelsior	one	4.95			1890	1898	2	1N7405	1138
10b	Mattress, excelsior and cotton (sea moss before 1903)	one	8.45	5.27	8.22	1894	1898	4	1N7421	1138

11a	Blanket, cotton	one	2.82	2.92	3.58	1894	1896	2	24N7162 1/4	569
11b	Blanket, part wool	one	4.32			1890	1897	3	24N7454	570
12	Bedsheet, cotton, double bed size	one	1.44	1.29	1.38	1890	1897	2	36N1306	578
13	Pillowcase, hemmed	one	0.38	0.38	0.42	1890	1897	1	36N1328	579
14a	Stove, heating, coal	one	10.90	13.01	19.70	1893	1897	3	22N691	1257
14b	Stove, cooking, gas (coal before 1902)	one	17.75			1892	1897	3	22N813	1242
15a	Ice chest	one	8.98	9.99	15.78	1892	1896	1	1L2805 1/3	1077c
15b	Standing refrigerator (ice box)	one	15.65			1892	1897	5	1L2820 1/3	1077c
16	Damask yard goods, 56–58 in. for table-cloth (linen to 1901, cotton 1901–18)	yard	0.85	1.52d	1.70d	1892	1896	2	36N2618	604
17a	Towel, cotton huck (linen, 1890–1902)	one	0.26	0.25	0.28	1890	1897	3	36N1714	613
17b	Towel, turkish	one	0.34			1890	1895	1	36N1976	614
18	Baby carriage (wood 1911–18, reed 1890–1910)	one	17.95	11.73	14.79	1890	1898	4	1N7915	271
19a	Sewing machine, hand power	one	12.25	11.05	24.44	1899	1900	1	26N154	557
19b	Sewing machine, foot power (drop head after 1895)	one	22.95			1890	1894	4	26N120	551

a From *Cost of Living in the United States*, BLS Bulletin 357. "Low" refers to the income class for which average expenditure per item was lowest; "average" refers to the average of all income classes. The item designation given in Bulletin 357 is usually broader than that shown here.

b The transition from Sears to Ward catalogues is counted as a link even if the price was the same from both houses and the item was otherwise identical.

c Priced from spring catalogues.

d Per tablecloth, not per yard.

TABLE D-2

Clothing[a]

Item No.	Description and Major Changes	Unit	1918 Price	Annual Expenditure per Article, 1918[b]		Series Begins	Ward Data End	Number of Links[c]	1918 Sears Catalogue	
				Low	Average				Number	Page
Man's										
1a	Union suit, combed cotton (before 1901, shirt and drawers)	one	$1.48			1890	1900	2	16L5117	320[d]
1b	Union suit, ribbed lisle (before 1901, shirt and drawers)	one	1.42	$1.41	$1.58	1897	1900	1	16L5150	321[d]
2a	Cap, winter, corduroy (wool cloth before 1912)	one	1.00	0.95	1.11	1890	1898	2	93N4622	394
3a	Hat, felt fedora (derby before 1898)	one	2.50	2.58	3.23	1890	1898	3	93N6104	391
3b	Hat, felt fedora	one	3.50			1898	none	3	93N6220	392
4	Overcoat, cloth, sheepskin lined	one	19.50	14.79	22.38	1896	1900	3	41N444	483
5a	Work pants (overalls before 1897)	pair	2.10	1.88	2.14	1890	1897	2	41N7391	502
5b	Overalls, denim	pair	2.25			1890	1897	3	41N7393	500
6a	Work shirt, chambray (cheviot before 1897)	one	1.00			1890	1897	1	33N664	398
6b	Work shirt, chambray (jersey before 1908)	one	1.29	1.09	1.31	1896	1901	3	33N650	398
6c	Dress shirt, cotton, no collar	one	1.35			1890	1901	3	33N216	404
7	Union suit, part wool (before 1898, shirt and drawers)	one	3.25	3.22	3.68	1890	1897	3	16N6010	349
8a	Nightshirt, muslin	one	1.19	1.08	1.27	1890	1896	2	33N908	374
8b	Nightshirt, flannelette	one	1.29			1896	1898	1	33N921	374
9a	Socks, cotton	pair	{0.26	0.24	0.28	1890	1897	3	86N2030	365
9b			0.27}			1896	1897	2	86N2047	365
10a	Shoes, work	pair	4.95	4.39	5.17	1898	none	3	15N4137	219
10b	Shoes, dress	pair	4.45			1890	1895	4	15N4108	215

No.	Item	Unit						Qty	Catalog No.	Ref.
11	Rubbers	pair	0.98	1.23	1.28	1890	1896	1	76N9128	235
12	Collar, celluloid	one	0.19	0.17	0.18	1890	1899	1	any style	388
13a	Necktie, silk	one	[0.45	0.46	0.61	1890	1898	2	33N8398	377
13b			0.55]			1890	1898	4	33N8339	377
Boy's										
14	Mackinaw or reefer, wool	one	9.50	5.67	7.35	1896	1897	3	40N2702	518
15	Knickerbockers, corduroy (knee pants before 1909)	pair	1.35	1.39	1.57	1890	1901	2	40L620	447[d]
16	Knickerbockers, all wool serge (knee pants before 1909, cassimere before 1899)	pair	2.45	1.64	2.19	1890	1907	3	40N2616	510
17	Union suit, cotton (shirt and drawers before 1908)	one	0.78	0.89	1.08	1895	1904	3	16L7510	313[d]
18a	Union suit, part wool (all wool shirt and drawers before 1897)	one	1.98	1.84	2.15	1890	1901	4	16N7110	342
18b	Union suit, part wool (shirt and drawers before 1901)	one	2.68			1896	1901	4	16N7335	343
19a	Stockings, cotton	pair	{0.33	0.32	0.36	1890	1898	1	86N2605	359
19b			0.38}			1890	1898	2	86N2608	359
20a	Shoes, high	pair	{2.69	2.89	3.57	1890	1900	7	15S5224	205
20b			3.49}			1890	1900	5	15N4924	202
Woman's										
21a	Corset	one	[1.98	1.75	2.35	1890	1895	8	18N235	254
21b			2.48]			1890	1896	6	18N205	253
22	Corset cover, knitted cotton	one	0.50	0.51	0.66	1903	none	1	16N6842	338
23a	Union suit, cotton, sleeveless	one	0.62	1.02	1.13	1896	1897	3	16L6872	316[d]
23b	Union suit, lisle (vests before 1892)	one	0.79			1890	1902	4	16L6868	317[d]

151

For notes to [a], [b], [c], and [d] see p. 152.

(continued)

TABLE D-2 (concluded)

Item No.	Description and Major Changes	Unit	1918 Price	Annual Expenditure per Article, 1918[b]		Series Begins	Ward Data End	Number of Links[c]	1918 Sears Catalogue	
				Low	Average				Number	Page
24	Stockings, cotton, fleece lined	pair	$0.27	$0.28	$0.37	1890	1897	4	86N2474	370
25a	Shoes, high	pair	{2.98	4.28	5.34	1890	1900	6	15N620	184
25b			{3.95					4	15N913	178
Girl's										
26a	Shoes, low	pair	{1.60	1.53	1.71	1904	none	none	15L7604	257[d]
26b			{1.35			1901	none	4	15L8480	260[d]
27a	Coat, winter, fur-like cloth	one	{4.98	3.98	4.63	1908	none	1	17N8817	39
27b			{3.98					2	17N8797	41
28	Underwaist	one	0.39	0.32	0.35	1894	1897	2	16N7074	340
Yard Goods and Trimmings										
29a	Wool serge	yard	{2.44			1893	1901	3	14NO 331	620
29b			{1.25			1890	1916	4	14NO 310	620
30	Gingham, checked or striped	yard	0.24			1890	1897	2	36N3230	584
31	Voile (dotted swiss before 1914)	yard	0.26			1890	1897	4	36N3079	600
32	Buttons, white pearl, 24-line	dozen	0.08			1890	1912	2	25N5078	660
33	Braid trim[e]	yard	0.02			1890	1897	6	25N3774	649
34	Lining, silk[e]	yard	1.05			1890	1912	3	14N8381	627

a This table excludes five items for which chain indexes were used. See text, p. 83.

b See note a under home furnishings. For man's items, the expenditures shown are those of husbands; for woman's items, those of wives; for boy's items, those of male children, 12 years and under 15 years; for girl's items, those of female children, 4 years and under 8 years.

c See note b under home furnishings.

d Priced from spring catalogues.

e These items enter into the composite price of a woman's wool suit before 1906. After 1906, this composite series is used only in the alternative version of the clothing index.

152

APPENDIX E—Composition of Indexes of Items Common to Wholesale and Retail Price Indexes

TABLE E-1

Basic Item	Description[a]		1918 Price[b]	
	Wholesale	Retail	Wholesale	Retail
Home Furnishings				
Carpet	Axminister, Lowell	Wool faced tapestry	c	c
		All-wool Brussels	c	c
Chair	Kitchen, hardwood	Dining room, hardwood	$0.97	$1.98
	Bedroom, oak rocker		1.63	
Table	Kitchen, hardwood base	Hardwood, drop leaf	2.74	6.85
Bedroom set	Iron bedstead, hardwood dresser, and washstand	Iron bedstead, oak dresser	31.84	24.10
Blanket	Cotton, 2 lbs. to the pair	Cotton, 4 lbs. to the pair	0.95	2.82
	Wool, 5 lbs. to the pair	40% wool, 5 lbs. to the pair	6.56	4.32
Sheet	Brown sheeting, Indian Head	Unbleached bedsheet, 81 × 86 in.	c	c
	Brown sheeting, Pepperell			
	Brown sheeting, Ware Shoals			
Clothing				
All wool dress goods, per yard	Storm serge, 50 in.	Storm serge, 54 in.	1.46	2.44
		Storm serge, 36 in.		1.25
Gingham, per yard	Amoskeag	Amoskeag, apron checks	0.18	0.24
Man's shoes, pair	Seamless Creedmores	Work shoe, Goodyear welt	1.51	4.95
	Vici calf, Goodyear welt	Gunmetal lace, Simplex welt	5.63	4.45
	Vici kid, Goodyear welt		5.44	
Woman's shoes, pair	Gunmetal button, McKay sewed	Black kid button, warm lined, McKay sole	3.71	2.98
		Black kid lace, low rubber heel		3.95
Man's cotton hose, pair	Combed yarn, black	Heavy carded yarn, black	0.16	0.26
		Black, undyed soles		0.27
Woman's cotton hose, pair	Full-fashioned, combed yarn	Heavy seamless, carded yarn, fleece lined	0.31	0.27
	Seamless, single thread		0.18	
Man's wool union suit	Merino, $33\frac{1}{3}$% wool, light weight	One-third wool, extra heavy weight	1.46	3.25

SOURCE: Sears, Roebuck and Company, Catalogue 137, Fall 1918 and BLS Bulletin 269, pp. 70–96 and 132–136.
a When more than one specific item is shown in either column, the series for that column is a simple average of relatives for the specific items.
b Prices are quoted per yard for yard goods, per pair for shoes and hosiery, and per item for all other items.
c Prices in sources cannot be reduced to comparable units.

153

APPENDIX F

Sources and Methods for Estimates of Rent Levels

THE sources and methods for computing average rent levels from newspaper data have been described in the text. This appendix will describe by years the budget studies and housing surveys used to make the rent-level comparisons shown in Table 36.

1918

The BLS budget study of 1918 has already been discussed in connection with the clothing and furniture indexes. The figures shown in Table 36 are obtained from the data on average annual expenditure on rent per year by cities in *Cost of Living in the United States*, BLS Bulletin 357, pp. 276–333. The data are given by income groups. We have used the data for income groups below $1,500 (for an explanation of this restriction, see notes 4 and 13 in Chapter 4). Annual rents for each of the three income groups were weighted by the number of families in the group, and the weighted average was converted to a monthly figure. Data for flats and apartments only were used in New York, Chicago, and Boston, and for both houses and flats and apartments in Cincinnati and St. Louis. The data on number of families by size and type of dwelling unit, from the same study and for the same income groups, provide the weights for the newspaper data. Therefore, the two sets of figures for average rent per month for 1918 shown in Table 36 apply to the same size distribution of dwelling units.

1909

The survey data for February 1909 are from Great Britain, Board of Trade, *Cost of Living in American Towns* (1911). Agents of the Board of Trade visited twenty-eight cities and, in each, visited a considerable number of working-class dwellings in various parts of the city. The number of dwelling units visited is not stated. For New York, rents and living conditions in more than forty buildings are described in

154

detail as examples; in most of these buildings several units are described.

The rents for each city are summarized in a table giving ranges of "predominant weekly rents of working-class dwellings," by rooms per unit. These ranges are stated in units of British currency per week; thus for New York, the range for three-room units is 9s. 7d. to 13s. 6d. When the ranges are converted to American currency at the rate of 2 cents to the penny[1] and multiplied by $4\frac{1}{3}$, they are seen to be ranges in dollars per month to the nearest dollar—thus, the range in the example given above becomes $10.00 to $14.00. We have used data for the sizes of units that our data and the Board of Trade data have in common. For these sizes, we have taken the midpoint of the range of dollars per month and divided by the number of rooms. These average rents per room were weighted by our weights for the various sizes as shown in Table 33. The weights for houses and apartments of the same size were combined, since the Board of Trade tables do not distinguish type of unit.

1907

The New York data for 1907 are from Robert Coit Chapin, *Standard of Living Among Working Men's Families in New York City* (1909), pp. 85 and 96. The study covered 391 families (291 in Manhattan and 100 in the Bronx, Brooklyn, and Queens). Enumerators tried to find families "with both parents living and 2 to 4 children under 16 years of age." Dependent families were excluded (*ibid.*, p. 28).

We have used the data on average annual rent per family by income class (*ibid.*, p. 85), which were restricted to 318 families with incomes between $600 and $1,099. The average annual rent for each class was weighted by the number of families in the class and the weighted average was converted to a monthly figure. Then, from the data given on page 96, we constructed a weighted average number of rooms per family for the same income classes. To get the figure shown in Table 36, the average monthly rent per family was divided by the average number of rooms per family.

1902

The New York data for 1902 are from New York City Tenement House Department, *First Report*, Vol. II (1904). This gives the results

[1] That is $4.80 to the pound, a convenient approximation to the par of $4.87 to the pound. For example, the study gives New York subway fares (then 5 cents) as $2\frac{1}{2}d$.

of a complete census of rented dwelling units in Manhattan and Brooklyn made in November and December 1902.[2]

Pages 12–23 give frequency distributions of tenement houses by average monthly rent per room, for the most part by 5 cent intervals, for the two boroughs separately. The distributions cover 38,732 tenement houses (buildings) having 380,618 tenements in Manhattan, and 32,894 tenement houses having 143,131 tenements in Brooklyn. We have computed the means of these two distributions and combined them, using the number of tenements (dwelling units) as weights. The mean rents per room for the two boroughs separately are $3.79 for Manhattan and $2.56 for Brooklyn.

1900

The Chicago data of 1900 are from City Homes Association, *Tenement Conditions in Chicago* (1901), p. 185. This work is the report of an investigation by a committee that included Jane Addams and Anita McCormick Blaine; the work of the enumerators was directed by Frank A. Fetter. Because the principal concern of the study was crowding and sanitary conditions, it was confined to three small districts representative of bad housing.

The table on rents (*ibid.*, p. 185) gives average rent per room for 420 apartments, divided into five classes by districts and predominant national or religious group (Italian, Jewish, mixed Italian and Jewish, Polish, and Bohemian). The number of apartments in each class is not given; we have shown, therefore, the simple average of the figures for the five classes. Because of the way in which the areas studied were selected, it is not surprising that the average rent is very low.

1893

The data for 1893 are from the *Seventh Special Report of the Commissioner of Labor, The Slums* (1894). This study was prepared by Commissioner Carroll D. Wright in compliance with a Congressional joint resolution of July 1892. It covers selected areas of the slums of Baltimore, Chicago, New York, and Philadelphia. The field work was done in April 1893. The population in 1893 of the areas covered

2 This report and several earlier reports use the word "tenement" to refer to a rented dwelling unit and "tenement house" to a building containing one or more such units. The present association of the word "tenement" with slums was absent, as shown by the inclusion in the tables of units renting for more than $50 a month.

(for our cities) was Chicago, 19,748; New York, 28,996; and Philadelphia, 17,060. The Chicago data are for part of the near West Side, and the New York data are for parts of lower Manhattan.

The tables on pages 595–600 of the *Seventh Special Report* give frequency distributions of tenements (dwelling units) by average weekly rent and number of rooms, to the nearest 5 cents. We have computed the means of the distributions for the room sizes used in our index and expressed them as monthly rents per room. These mean monthly rents per room for units of each size were weighted by the weights of Table 33.

The average rents per room shown by the *Seventh Special Report* are surprisingly high for slum areas. This may be explained, in part, by the fact that the areas selected are close to the central business districts. The New York data are confined to Manhattan, and we know that Brooklyn rents in 1902 were much lower than Manhattan rents. Another possible explanation of the high average rent per room is the large number of persons to a room. (The New York data show more sleeping rooms with three or four occupants than with one or two. One room had thirty-one occupants and only one outside window; one room had ninety-two occupants!) The New York data are largely for units with only two or three rooms; however, four-room units were common in Philadelphia and Chicago.

1891

The Boston data of 1891 are from the *Twenty-second Annual Report* of the Massachusetts Bureau of Labor Statistics (1892). This report gives the results of a complete census of rented dwelling units (tenements) in the city of Boston taken during 1891. The census covers 71,665 occupied tenements. The use of the term "tenement" is again very broad; the tables include a unit of thirteen rooms renting for $333.33 a month. Page 512 of the *Report* gives the average monthly rent per unit by number of rooms. We have selected the sizes used in our index, converted the averages to rents per room, and weighted these by the weights for the various room sizes used in our index.

Index

Addams, Jane, 156
Agricultural implements industry, omission of, in industry estimates, 40
Agriculture, *see* Farm products
Aldrich Report, 66–67
American Assembly, 122n
Automobile industry, omission of, in industry estimates, 40

Baking industry: unionization in, 20; wages in, 11n, 25
Baltimore Gas and Electric Company, 106n
Barger, Harold, 94n
Bean, Louis H., 13n
Bethlehem Steel Corporation, wage series, 60–62
Biases in wage data, 39, 40, 56, 67
Blaine, Anita McCormick, 156
Blank, David M., 96n, 105n
Boot and shoe industry: definition of, 140; establishments and workers in sample, 22, 58; hours of work in, 26, 28, 36, 42, 47; money wages in, 11, 25, 26, 43, 47, 52, 56, 65, 67; real wages in, 124, 125; workers per establishment, 21, 27
Boston: rent index, 97; rent levels, 102, 157
Bowden, Witt, 19n, 38n
Bowley, A. L., 15n, 16n
Brady, Dorothy S., 88n
Brissenden, Paul F., 23, 24n
Building trades, wage series in, 8, 19
Bureau of Labor Statistics: data from, 6, 10–12, 21–23, 27, 28, 39, 43, 51, 56–63, 65, 83; indexes of, 9, 10, 66, 79–81, 86, 90, 91, 100, 104, 105, 107, 116

Carpet industry, *see* Textile industry (all)
Catalogues, *see* Mail-order catalogues
Census of Manufactures, data from: 6, 56; employment, 29–31, 33, 40, 41; 34–36; gas prices, 109; operating time of establishments, wages, 18, 23, 39, 41, 57
Chain-link indexing procedure, 83–85, 88, 89, 108
Chapin, Robert Coit, 102, 104n
Chemicals industry, omission of, in industry estimates, 41
Chicago: rent index, 97; rent levels, 102

Chow, Gregory C., 98n
Cincinnati: rent index, 97; rent levels, 102
Cincinnati Gas and Electric Company, 106n
City Homes Association (Chicago), 102, 156
Clothing: in cost-of-living index, 74–75; items chosen for cost-of-living index, 82, 91–93, 150–152
  price indexes: 4, 11, 75, 85–87, 90; bias in, 119; definitional problems in, 79; retail and wholesale, comparison of 91–93, 95, 153; weights for, 10, 87–89, 114, 115, 117
Clothing industry: hours of work in, 37; omission of, in industry estimates, 40; wages in, 11, 25
Coal, as component of fuel and light index, 105, 106, 109–112
Coal industry: exclusion from wage estimates, 31n; food expenditures of workers in, 78; wages in, 23
Coke industry, food expenditures of workers in, 78
Commissioner of Labor: Sixth and Seventh Annual Reports, 77, 78, 111; Seventh Special Report, 156–157; Eighteenth Annual Report, 6, 11, 77, 78, 114, 115; Nineteenth Annual Report, 22, 43, 57, 69
Commons, J. R., 59n
Connecticut, wage statistics from, 23–73, 134–135
Consolidated Edison Company of New York, 106n
Consumer Price Index, 13, 116
Cost-of-living index: 4, 5, 11, 74–120; bias in, 119; components, 74, 75; Douglas, *see* Douglas, Paul H., cost-of-living index; errors in measurement of, 16; Hansen, 10
Cotton goods industry: definition of, 41, 56, 137; establishments and workers in sample, 22, 41, 57; hours of work in, 26, 28, 36, 42–44; money wages in, 11, 25–26, 41, 43–44, 51, 57, 64–67, 78; movement of wage series in, 57, 59; real wages in, 124–125; workers per establishment in, 21, 27; *see also* Textiles (all)
Cyclical fluctuations, 17

159

HD
4975   Rees, Albert
R4   Real wages in manufactu –
         ring.